Governance Series

Governance is the process of effective coordination whereby an organization or a system guides itself when resources, power and information are widely distributed. Studying governance means probing the pattern of rights and obligations that underpins organizations and social systems, understanding how they coordinate their parallel activities and maintain their coherence, exploring the sources of dysfunction, and suggesting ways to redesign organizations whose governance is in need of repair.

The series welcomes a range of contributions—from conceptual and theoretical reflections, ethnographic and case studies, and proceedings of conferences and symposia, to works of a very practical nature—that deal with problems or issues on the governance front. The series publishes works both in French and in English.

The Governance Series is part of the publications division of the Centre on Governance and of the Graduate School of Public and International Affairs at the University of Ottawa. This is the 27th volume published in the series. The Centre on Governance and the Graduate School of Public and International Affairs also publish a quarterly electronic journal, www.optimumonline.ca.

Editorial Committee

The published titles in the series are listed at the end of this book.

The Case for
Decentralized
Federalism

edited by
Ruth Hubbard &
Gilles Paquet

UNIVERSITY OF OTTAWA PRESS
OTTAWA

University of Ottawa Press
542 King Edward Avenue
Ottawa, ON K1N 6N5
www.press.uottawa.ca

The University of Ottawa Press acknowledges with gratitude the support extended to its publishing list by Heritage Canada through its Book
Publishing Industry Development Program, by the Canada Council
for the Arts, by the Canadian Federation for the Humanities and Social
Sciences through its Aid to Scholarly Publications Program, by the
Social Sciences and Humanities Research Council, and by the University
of Ottawa.

We also gratefully acknowledge the Centre on Governance at the
University of Ottawa and Invenire4 Ltd., whose financial support has
contributed to the publication of this book.

LIBRARY AND ARCHIVES CANADA CATALOGUING IN PUBLICATION

The case for decentralized federalism /
edited by Ruth Hubbard & Gilles Paquet.

(Governance series, ISSN 1487-3052; 27)
Companion volume to: The case for centralized federalism
Includes bibliographical references and index.
ISBN 978-0-7766-0745-0

1. Decentralization in government—Canada.
2. Federal government—Canada.
I. Hubbard, Ruth, 1942- II. Paquet, Gilles, 1936–
III. Series: Governance series (Ottawa, Ont.); 27

JL86.D39C38 2010   352.2'830971   C2010-902834-1

Institutions have a future...people have no future. People have hope.

—Ivan Illich

Table of Contents

Contributors

Bélanger, Gérard
Gérard Bélanger is Professor in the Department of Economics at Laval University.

Courchene, Thomas J.
Thomas J. Courchene is Jarislowsky-Deutsch Professor of Economics and Financial Policy, School of Policy Studies at Queen's University, and Senior Scholar at the Institute for Research on Public Policy.

Gilbert, Marie-Christine
Marie-Christine Gilbert is a doctoral candidate in the School of Political Studies at the University of Ottawa.

Hubbard, Ruth
Ruth Hubbard is Senior Research Fellow at the Centre on Governance at the University of Ottawa, and Senior Partner in Invenire.

Paquet, Gilles
Gilles Paquet is Professor Emeritus at the Telfer School of Management, Senior Research Fellow at the Centre on Governance of the University of Ottawa, and Senior Partner in Invenire.

Peach, Ian
Ian Peach was Special Advisor to the Office of the Federal Interlocutor for Metis and non-Status Indians, Indian and Northern Affairs Canada, at the time his chapter was prepared.

Rocher, François
François Rocher is the Director of the School of Political Studies at the University of Ottawa.

Segal, Hugh D.
The Hon. Hugh D. Segal is a Senior Research Fellow at McMillan LLP, Senior Fellow and Chair of the Policy Forum at the Queen's School of Policy Studies and a member of the Senate of Canada.

Foreword

This volume is one of a pair of books published in the Governance Series by the University of Ottawa Press as the outcome of the Federalism Redux Project. These two books provide the requisite vocabulary and schemes of arguments likely to be useful for those who would like to articulate the best case that can be made for centralized and decentralized federalism respectively.

This particular volume makes the case for decentralization while the companion volume, edited by Gordon DiGiacomo and Maryantonett Flumian, makes the case for centralization.

The Federalism Redux Project is aimed at presenting the best case for each position in the most analytically sound and the least ideologically corrupted ways. It is for the reader to determine whether the books have delivered on their promise, and whether, as a result, someone who has worked carefully through both books is likely to be persuaded more effectively by one or the other.

Our main objective is to get away from the continuous whining about petty grievances or the doldrums of institutional plumbing, and to stimulate a serious discussion about the best way to initiate an important and useful conversation about federalism in Canada, and on how it might best serve Canada going forward. We invite readers to communicate with the authors and editors in order to make their views and criticisms known.

It is the intention of the Editor in Chief of *Optimumonline* at www.optimumonline.ca to provide a forum for a broad range of views on these books in forthcoming issues.

We would like to thank the Centre on Governance at the University of Ottawa: its various forms of support for the Federalism Redux Project are gratefully acknowledged.

Ruth Hubbard and Gilles Paquet
Gordon DiGiacomo and Maryantonett Flumian

Federalism as a Philosophy of Governance

Ruth Hubbard and Gilles Paquet

> *...our Fathers of Confederation possessed many fine qualities
> and talents. I can guarantee, however, that clairvoyance was
> not among them....*
> —Allan Gregg

Governance has been defined as effective coordination when
power, resources and information are widely distributed.

Federalism is a philosophy of governance, a social technology, and a mode of public governance. It proposes ways
to cope with contextual diversity and cultural pluralism
through a division of the work of public governing among
different levels of government. It strikes a compromise
between centralization and decentralization—with each
level of government being sovereign in its own world, but
of necessity obliged to accommodate the partners through
a variety of arrangements more or less formal—vertical,
horizontal and transversal. The polycentric governance that
ensues is seen as doing much to protect the citizen from the
natural propensity of government to centralize.

Traditionally, federalism has often been approached by
lawyers and public administration specialists strictly in
plumbing terms: as a set of mechanisms to allocate rights
and responsibilities among levels of territorial (local, provincial, federal) or 'national' administration. This has diverted

attention from the central concern: ascertaining the ways and means by which the citizens of an advanced democracy can steer and steward their society (both directly and indirectly) so that it thrives in the future.

The surface-level discussions in good currency have produced a Manichean literature built on different sets of propositions.

A first set is characterized by an argument generally based on three more or less explicit propositions: someone must be in charge; the senior level government is best equipped to do the job; and if hierarchical leadership is not exerted, unacceptable governance failures ensue.

The second set is characterized by the propositions that nobody is fully in charge; that, depending on the issue domain, different levels of government (or some private or social concern) may be better equipped to take the lead; and that this 'heterarchy' generates workable governance.

Readers will undoubtedly recognize those sets of propositions percolating through the two volumes of the Federalism Redux Project.

Our approach in the present volume is squarely built on the second set of propositions and defends the view that the objective should be as much decentralization as possible but as much centralization as necessary. It is our view that decentralized federalism constitutes, through the development of a philosophy of polycentric governance and the design and operations of confederally-inspired decentralized structures, the most efficient, equitable and practical way to govern a pluralist and heterogeneous country, while preserving autonomy and liberty, and ensuring resilience and innovativeness.

Federalism as palimpsest

As a mode of governance, federalism is as much an idea and a *manière de voir* as a regime of public administration proper. We regard it as a living perspective on a Canadian reality that has many faces. Consequently, we recognize that it has evolved through time, and will continue to evolve as its users' perspectives change.

As Allan Gregg mentions in the epigraph, those who wrote our founding documents were not clairvoyant: nobody is. They put forward a first draft of an arrangement that was meant to evolve through time, has done so, and continues to do so in response to shifting realities. Not only have the basic objectives come to be sought by different means, but the very objectives pursued have also changed. This has affected the allocation of rights and responsibilities. At any one time, Canadian federalism is therefore very much like a palimpsest: the sort of parchment on which scripts are etched and scraped to allow the etching of a new message. Since the old messages are only partly erased and leave visible traces, the superimposed messages and partly scraped layers of messages make for difficult reading and interpretation.

In this introductory chapter, we acknowledge first the diverse and pluralistic context that has called for the use of polycentric governance in modern societies, and led to a governing apparatus based on the allocation of decision making to a multiplicity of loci rather than to any single central potentate. Second, we question some of the assumptions on which the case for centralization is based. Finally we provide an overview of the different ways in which the various authors of the chapters in this volume have made the case for decentralized federalism.

The case for polycentricity

Federalism is a philosophy of polycentric governance based on the recognition that a complex and variegated system (where the interactions are nested into many games operating simultaneously at different scales of aggregation) may not be necessarily and optimally governed from a single centre. Consequently, it has been found legitimate to speculate on the best way to approach the problem of designing rules to ensure effective polycentric governance.

Even a relatively homogeneous population must face somewhat different and changing circumstances as it grows. Consequently, the governing apparatus must evolve on the basis of the continuous flow of new information emerging from this changing environment. So it is rather difficult and inefficient to rely on the limited information available to a single centralized governing unit to handle all public affairs. Some devolution has proved useful in most evolving contexts.

The difficulties are even more daunting when one is faced with a variety of territorially differentiated or deeply diverse groups, who may have different notions of the good. In such cases, a central governing unit may be truly incapable of effectively gathering and marshalling the whole array of information necessary to govern the social system aptly.

Federalism is therefore a way of both ensuring that decision making in different issue domains will be tailored to the differentiated terrain, and accommodating the needs and aspirations of diverse groups (and even their desire of self-government in particular matters). Additionally, federalism is a good way to avoid the danger of tyranny by any particular group. Because of the multiplicity of loci for decision making, it also provides greater opportunity for experimentation and innovation as different groups may try to tackle similar difficulties in different ways (Kohr 1941).

In a federal system like Canada that contains both region-based and culture-based groups, the nature of the demands or felt needs for particular powers at the non-central level may vary markedly. Indeed, there has been a major difference between the sort of demands that have been heard in the world of territorial federalism and that are based on the need for devolution to the junior levels of government in the name of proximity and efficiency, and those that have been heard in the world of multinational federalism and that are based on the requirements of identity recognition.

In the first case, some asymmetry between what might be devolved to large and small provinces or to large or small cities in the name of efficiency can be accommodated more easily. In the second case, the whole notion of asymmetry entails a sense of special status that has been found unpalatable by many who have been insistent on the fundamental equality of all citizens. This is the reason why various arrangements for policing, for instance, in different parts of the country have been easy to accept, while the notions of Quebec as a *société distincte* or of Aboriginals as 'citizens plus' (i.e., citizens with certain privileges not afforded to other citizens) have been such a hard sell.

The diffraction of modern society has had major impacts (Paquet 2005, chapter 13).

First, it poses numerous intractable challenges to unitary governing bodies. Even with the best of intentions, it is quite difficult to ensure that all the varied points of view are fully acknowledged and appropriately weighted in collective decision making. Aggregating such intractable challenges in macro-baskets, allowing for some horse-trading, is clever but not always helpful. It may lead to certain expedient and opportunistic balancing acts at the higher level, but such aggregation of social choices does not necessarily lead to optimal choices, or to consistent and fair choices, or even to choices that take diversity seriously.

Second, it generates different sorts of conflicts between or among factions that are not necessarily resolvable in the same ways. For instance, one must distinguish between routine 'distributional issues' that can be dealt with by discussion and negotiation, and 'categorical conflicts' that cannot be sorted out by debates and negotiations, because things such as identities "cannot be changed by rational arguments" (Fleiner 2001: 33).

These impacts impose certain constraints on the design of a workable governance system.

First, they raise serious questions about the possibility of even any unitary government being able to provide reasonable guidance on the sole basis of the rule of law. Therefore, it has led to much interest in federal systems that appear to be capable of resolving problems at a less aggregated level, by maintaining a diversity of 'rules of the game'.

Second, it suggests that some issues are not resolvable at all except at the 'community of meaning' level. Indeed, deep diversity generates numerous 'categorical conflicts': identities are based on a mix of objective and subjective realities that cannot be transformed by discussion. One does not become a Croat in the same manner as one changes one's view about income redistribution.

Third, deep diversity also calls for a modification in the modes of reconciliation of the various discourses. While there has been much use made of rights and *le droit* in the past, this is an orthopedic tool that has the knack of ossifying power relations in absolute ways. This may not be as effective a method of reconciliation in the dynamic context of present day diversity. Softer and subtler institutional forms of power-sharing or collaborative governance have the merit of allowing for some softer and more balanced processes to ensure that the voices of a variety of groups are going to be heard in specific terrains.

The required governance principles and tools are not easily designed, for they call for a partitioning of both the 'governance terrain' and the 'issues terrain' to provide acceptable arrangements of different sorts according to the nature of the issues, and of the stakeholders. Yet these principles and tools can be designed.

Assumptions challenged

In general for the authors of this volume, there are three sets of traditional assumptions that must be confronted:

a. the assumptions underpinning the "liberal constitutional project" (Carter 1998) that there is a need for central control;

b. the assumption that a bottom-up federalism is unworkable, and that it is impossible to design a legitimate and effective chaordic (i.e., mixed chaos/order, decentralized/centralized) system; and

c. the assumption that one cannot accommodate a variety of singular communities in the body politic, and therefore that building on the notion of *citoyens sans qualités* is a necessary detour.

These assumptions have been challenged before, but they have proved quite resilient.

Stephen Carter has made the point that the "liberal constitutional project" (built on the presumption that central government is "more likely than anybody else to find the answers that are right") is, in a powerful sense, anti-democratic, and anti-communitarian (Carter 1998: 20). It is based on the foundation that the views of the people are irrelevant except when they happen to be in support of the liberal constitutional project, in which case they are crucial (Ibid., 21).

The assumption that no governance system can function without central control is widely held and is best expounded by Dror (1997, 2001) and Jaques (2002) as an iron rule of living organizations. It posits the need for some constraints to be defined in order for a freedom-based organization to avoid floundering and collapsing. This body of doctrine has a deeply-attached following among people who prefer "centralized explanations" (Resnick 1994).

The second set of assumptions flows directly from the first, but complements it in a fundamental way and may be regarded, in part, as an enriched corollary. It suggests that no fully decentralized solution is likely to be viable, but it also adds that one cannot mix centralization and decentralization, state and market, order and chaos.

The first portion of these two assertions raises questions about the process of emergence itself, and has been effectively countered in recent work by Holland (1998). The second portion of these assertions—about the impossibility of effectively mixing elements of centralization and decentralization, state and market, order and chaos—has been regarded as a categorical imperative by Jacobs (1992). She has argued that mixing systems that are defined by different syndromes could only generate "monstrous hybrids". This argument is entirely spurious as we have shown elsewhere (Hubbard and Paquet 2002). Bottom-up chaordic organizations (mixing chaos and order) have proved workable, viable and effective (Hock 1999).

The third set of assumptions is more difficult to unplug. But it is also a derivative of the other two sets in the sense that the need for centralization and the so-called impos-

sibility of mixed institutions must entail a degree of
inability to take into account the variety of singular communities generated by a deeply diverse context. For its
devotees, this difficulty is conveniently ascribed both to
the large number of such communities, and to the coef-
ficient of rigidity of many "identity groups" (Piore 1995).
This is the argument that is used to insist on the sole basis
of the *citoyens sans qualités*—accepting to deal only with
citizens as devoid of any particular quality or characteristic—in constructing our political apparatus. Yet one cannot see how a pluralist political system can ignore such
diversity and not take these singular communities seriously (Agamben 2000).

These three sets of assumptions have polluted most
debates about Canadian federalism. They presume a 'natural' dominance of centralization and a need for control, the
impossibility of building bottom-up structures or mitigating
the 'malefits' of centralized organizations by mixed forms of
organizations, and the need to ignore singular communities
simply because they cannot be effectively taken into account
by a rigid uniformity-driven system.

A reframing of our federalism must be based on the con-
verse of these assumptions: the primacy of decentralization
as a design principle; the possibility of constructing hybrid
and baroque organizations to ensure that effective coordination ensues; and the requirement that singular communities
be afforded a requisite voice through flexible instruments
like regimes.

The case for decentralized federalism is made

In this volume, a number of colleagues have made a case
for decentralized federalism using quite dissimilar lines of
attack, and (implicitly or explicitly) challenging the assumptions set out above to varying degrees.

The first three papers present a positive analysis of Canadian federalism that leads, through various pathways, to
support the case for decentralization.

Thomas J. Courchene sets the table nicely by putting the matter in historical perspective, and by spelling out the various dimensions of the problems that Canadian federalism has successfully tackled by creatively crafting decentralized arrangements that have had the knack of becoming pan-Canadian.

Ian Peach approaches the problem as a practitioner of intergovernmental relations who has participated in this craft for quite a while. He argues for decentralization on the basis of the local communities having a better understanding of the nature of the challenges Canadians are facing, a keener awareness of the costs of inaction, and a greater ability to develop policy innovations.

Gérard Bélanger deals with the issue through a public choice lens. He analyzes both the centrifugal and centripetal forces at work in a federation, and his economist's perspective leads him to cautiously support the disposition toward decentralization that has evolved both historically and practically, because it is more likely to underpin competition—the key driver, in his view—that supports necessary innovation.

The next three papers are more normative and frame their perspectives in terms of different strategies to ensure satisfactory polycentric governance.

Hugh Segal argues forcefully for a philosophy of subsidiarity and the containment of the federal power to spend as major building blocks of the foundation of the Canadian confederal accord, and shows how the dynamics of robust subsidiarity strengthen the very rootedness of our citizenship.

François Rocher and Marie-Christine Gilbert argue that federalism and decentralization are co-constitutive notions. They challenge the often-repeated Ottawa slogan about the Canadian federation being one of the most decentralized in the world, and show that this is not the case. They make the case for a rekindling of a confederal culture and a re-federalization of Canadian federalism that would dramatically decentralize its operations. They also indicate the obstacles to be expected and that would have to be overcome on this difficult road.

Ruth Hubbard and Gilles Paquet focus on the central importance of variety in a federation, and debunk arguments claiming that decentralization is costly, unworkable, unfair, etc. as unpersuasive. They recognize that there are blockages to the implementation of a scheme like this—rooted as it is in social learning and 'open source'—and suggest ways in which such impediments could be overcome.

In conclusion, it is argued that whatever might be the broad objectives pursued (nation building *à la* Courchene, effectiveness *à la* Peach, competition as driver *à la* Bélanger, subsidiarity *à la* Segal, a true confederal culture *à la* Rocher and Gilbert or innovation, and open-source social learning *à la* Hubbard and Paquet), federalism remains a work in progress, an on-going baroque experiment in regime-building in which the centrality of decentralization is and will remain paramount.

References

Agamben, Giorgio 2000. *Means without Ends—Notes on Politics.* Minneapolis, MN: The University of Minnesota Press.

Carter, Stephen L. 1998. *The Dissent of the Governed.* Cambridge, MA: Harvard University Press.

Dror, Yehezkel 1997. "Delta-type Senior Civil Service for the 21st Century." *International Review of Administrative Sciences,* 63: 1: 7–23.

Dror, Yehezkel 2001. *The Capacity to Govern.* London: Frank Cass.

Fleiner, Thomas 2001. "Facing Diversity." *International Social Science Journal,* 53: 167: 33–40.

Hock, Dee 1999. *Birth of the Chaordic Age.* San Francisco, CA: Berrett-Koehler Publishers.

Holland, John H. 1998. *Emergence.* Reading, MA: Addison-Wesley.

Hubbard, Ruth and Gilles Paquet 2002. "Ecologies of governance and institutional metissage." www.optimumonline.ca, 31: 4: 25–34.

Jacobs, Jane 1992. *Systems of Survival.* New York: Random House.

Jaques, Elliott 2002. *The Life and Behavior of Living Organisms.* London: Praeger.

Kohr, Hans 1941. "Disunion now: A Plea for a Society based upon Small Autonomous Units." *The Commonweal,* 26 September.

Paquet, Gilles 2005. *The New Geo-governance*. Ottawa: The University of Ottawa Press.

Piore, Michael J. 1995. *Beyond Individualism*. Cambridge, MA: Harvard University Press.

Resnick, Michael 1994. *Turtles, Termites and Traffic Jams*. Cambridge, MA: The MIT Press.

Part I:
The Positive Case

Federalism, Decentralization and Canadian Nation Building

Chapter 1

Thomas J. Courchene

Introduction[1]

Federations come in all varieties: some are parliamentary (Canada, Australia), others are presidential (United States, Mexico); some have two constituted levels of government (Canada), others include municipal/local governments in their constitutions (Mexico, Germany); some are common-law federations (Canada, Australia, United States), others are civil-law federations (Germany, Austria); some have triple-E senates (United States, Argentina), others have appointed senates (Canada) and still others have upper chambers that are 'houses of the sub-national governments' (Germany); some are highly centralized (Australia, Germany), others are decentralized (Canada, Switzerland), and so on. In all cases, however, federalism is a combination of self rule and shared rule for the constituted levels of government.

The obvious starting point of any analysis of the relationship between decentralization and federalism is the constitutional division of powers. However, this static or legal degree of decentralization may not correspond with the actual degree of decentralization. In part at least, this is because the actual positioning of a federation along a centralization-decentralization spectrum will also be a function of many other factors, including the federal characteristics or trade-offs mentioned above.

For example, regardless of the division of powers, a uniformly civil-law federation will be more centralized than will a uniformly common-law federation (Fleiner 2010). In other words, to an important extent, the degree of centralization or decentralization is also a policy and societal instrument, one that can be called upon to accommodate the underlying nature of the federation and/or to achieve deeper societal goals. Indeed, and as the title indicates, the ensuing analysis will attempt to demonstrate that decentralization has played and will continue to play an absolutely pivotal role in our collective journey toward Canadian nation building.

The chapter proceeds as follows. First, it presents the analytical rationales for decentralization and, in particular, for decentralized federations. The next section deals with the constitutional, institutional and political/policy determinants of Canadian decentralization. On the constitutional front, for example, the Judicial Committee of the Privy Council (JCPC) shifted its initial focus from "peace, order and good government" (POGG) as the effective residual clause toward "property and civil rights" (Section 92 (13)), especially after the landmark 1937 Labour Convention decision. On the institutional front, the lack of any provincial representation in our central governing institutions meant that the provincial premiers would fill this void. On the political/policy front, the focus is, *inter alia*, on the Charter. The section concludes with a discussion of process vs. structure in terms of the *de facto* division of powers. The following section, entitled "Centralization-Decentralization, Asymmetry and *Deux Nations*", focuses on selected events leading up to the House of Commons proclamation that "the Québécois form a nation in a united Canada". Included here are the implementation of the Quebec personal income tax; opting out, Section 94 and, of course, *deux nations*. The next section, "Is Decentralization Endogenous?", addresses the issue of whether decentralization is an independent driver with its own internal dynamic or whether it may better be viewed as an accommodative instrument responding to deeper societal values and forces. After a review of several developed federations, the endogeneity thesis seems credible. A brief conclusion completes the chapter.

Decentralization as political and economic efficiency

The role of this section is to focus on decentralization as an instrument that advances economic efficiency (defined to include what has come to be called 'competitive federalism') as well as political efficiency (defined to include both democracy/accountability and 'taming leviathan').

Economic efficiency

The obvious launch point is the efficiency argument for a decentralized public sector. Although penned nearly forty years ago, Wallace Oates' 1972 *Fiscal Federalism* still merits quotation in this context:

> ...a decentralized public sector possesses several economically desirable characteristics. First, it provides a means by which the levels of consumption of some public goods can be tailored to the preferences of subsets of the society. In this way economic efficiency is enhanced by providing an allocation of resources that is more responsive to the tastes of consumers. Second, by promoting increased innovation over time and by providing competitive pressures to induce local governments to adopt the most efficient techniques of production, decentralization may increase both static and dynamic efficiency in the production of public goods (Oates 1972: 13).

Along related lines:

> Decentralization may, moreover, result in greater experimentation and innovation in the production of public goods. With a large number of independent producers of a good, one might expect a variety of approaches ... that,

in the long run, promise greater technical progress in modes of providing these goods and services (Ibid.,12).

Readers will recognize that this exactly describes the role that Saskatchewan played in the evolution of Medicare. More generally, federalism allows the flexibility and creativity of the market to come into play in the production of public goods and services. This is why the term competitive federalism has come to apply to this competition among the provinces.

To be sure, competitive federalism has its detractors. The typical concern is that competition among provinces could lead to the proverbial 'race to the bottom'. A good example of this occurred when Ottawa devolved succession duties to the provinces: they rather promptly reduced these duties to zero. It was clearly a mistake to devolve this tax to the provinces since it became captive to a negative-sum, cross-province competition for rich golden-agers. However, in *Racing to the Bottom* (Harrison 2006), the conclusions on this score tend to run in the opposite direction, namely that the competitive race is often to the top. This is demonstrably the case in terms of the climate change file: California and British Columbia are leading their respective federations on the environmental front, and in this they are well in front of their respective national governments.

Drawing from the work of Weingast (1995) relating to market-preserving federalism, McKinnon (1997) outlines the conditions under which sub-national (horizontal) competition can be welfare and efficiency enhancing. These conditions are four-fold: monetary separation (no financial bailout for governments); fiscal separation (no fiscal bailouts from the central government); freedom of interprovincial/interstate commerce (an internal economic union); and unrestricted public choice (tax and expenditure autonomy at the sub-national level). The first two conditions ensure that there are 'hard' monetary and budget constraints and the third condition prevents governments from fragmenting the economic union and/or legislating in a discriminatory manner. Within this context, interprovincial competition is benign, efficient and welfare enhancing, and leads to the positive results aired in the earlier quotes from Wallace Oates.

The principle of subsidiarity and the centralization-decentralization spectrum

As commonly understood, the principle of subsidiarity posits that, other things being equal, powers and programs should be assigned/located to the lowest level of government that can effectively implement these powers/programs, again for all the reasons indicated by Oates as well as for reasons related to enhancing democracy, accountability and citizen engagement. Moreover, if one defines the new global order as I do, namely a combination of globalization and the knowledge/information revolution (Courchene 2001), then the knowledge/information component argues strongly for increasing the extent of decentralization. This is because the associated tele-computational developments allow for much greater coordination and more ability to access and integrate relevant data and information at progressively lower levels of government than has hitherto been the case. In turn, this means that it is possible to "push down to the local level more power and revenues than ever before" (Friedman 1999: 293).

However, there is a flip side to the subsidiarity principle: in policy areas where externalities or policy spillovers exist, these policy areas should be transferred up the jurisdictional hierarchy to that level where the spillovers can be addressed or internalized. Whereas the knowledge/information component of the new global order argues, as noted, for transferring powers downwards, the globalization or 'ultra-mobility' component, where relevant, argues for transferring powers upwards. The interesting and important caveat here is that internalizing externalities need not imply passing provincial activities upwards to Ottawa; internalization can also be accomplished at the pan-provincial level. Indeed, this is one of the key rationales for the Council of the Federation: to perform the requisite overarching coordination that allows the provinces to design and deliver selected programs that otherwise would call for centralization. The recent (2009) Council of the Federation-driven agreement on ensuring full cross-province mobility of credentials and occupations is a case in point.

At this juncture, it is important to emphasize that in numerable cases where policy spillovers required either passing powers upwards or finding creative ways to internalize these externalities, Canada opted for the latter. Often the exercise of the federal spending power was called upon for the task. A good example here was the use of federal cost-sharing for welfare (in the context of the Canada Assistance Plan (CAP)), replete with prohibiting residence requirements. In tandem, cost-sharing and no residency requirements respectively allowed the provinces to develop more generous welfare programs and to ensure that these individual provincial welfare programs could be integrated into a version of a national system. The key point here is that both Ottawa and the provinces cooperated to ensure that the requisite pan-Canadian requirements were achieved in a way that allowed our decentralized design and delivery of welfare to be maintained and enriched.

A further reason for linking subsidiarity with the centralization-decentralization spectrum in the title of this section is the following: when reference is made to decentralization in Canada, it virtually always means transferring powers from Ottawa to the provinces and not from Ottawa and the provinces to the municipal level. Why should subsidiarity stop with the provinces? Any new global-order version of subsidiarity would suggest that many activities can and should be passed down to the city/municipal level. The reality is that, in terms of access to own revenues and to expenditure responsibilities, Canada's cities rank among the most constrained anywhere in the developed world. This is most unfortunate because the new era has led to the economic, political and even democratic ascendancy of cities, especially for what have come to be called global city regions. If our cities remain both fiscally weak and jurisdictionally constitutionless, the likelihood is that they will fall short of their new global-order potential (Courchene 2007). Here is another area where Canada remains too centralized, not too decentralized.

One can take this further and suggest that the lack of meaningful decentralization is one of the reasons why the recognized potential for democracy to flourish at the local level has not materialized in Canada. Simply put, it is difficult for citizens to be enthusiastic about local democracy as long as city politicians are largely administrators of responsibilities and policies that are legislated (and funded) elsewhere. Much better, if this is the case, to join the city politicians and engage in rent-seeking at the provincial and federal doorsteps. However, were there greater political autonomy involving enhanced responsibilities and greater access to tax revenues, the stage would then be set for more meaningful citizen engagement since much more would be at stake at the city level. In effect, the result would be more local autonomy and more democratic governance.

With this as backdrop, attention is now directed to the origins of our decentralized federation.

Decentralization: constitutional, institutional and political determinants

The division of powers and "property and civil rights" (Section 92 (13))

Accepted wisdom is that our Fathers of Confederation, fully aware of the ongoing American Civil War at the time of the 1864 Charlottetown and Quebec conferences, did not want to create a constitution embodying a degree of decentralization that could lead to similar 'states' rights' movements on our side of the border. Presumably, this was among the reasons for including the "peace, order and good government" preamble to listing of federal powers in Section 91 of the *British North America (BNA) Act* (henceforth, *Constitution Act, 1867*) with the intention of it serving the role as the "residual clause".

However, there were several other factors, some societal, some constitutional, some geographical, etc., that conspired to ensure that Canada would likely end up as a decentralized federation. The most important was that Confederation was the union of three English-speaking, common-law colonies and Quebec with its own language, legal system and culture. Of and by itself, this was probably enough to tilt the balance toward a decentralist federation rather than, say, a centralized federation or even, as some of the Fathers of Confederation wished, a unitary state. This decentralist thrust was powerfully buttressed by the inclusion of Section 92 (13) "property and civil rights" in the list of exclusive provincial powers. This wording initially appeared in the *Quebec Act* (1774) and was carried over to the *BNA Act*, where it was deemed, at least by Quebec and eventually by the JCPC to essentially encompass what we would now call the social envelope as well as aspects of ownership/property (from which provincial securities regulation, for example, initially drew its *raison d'être*). Indeed, such is the potential sweep of Section 92 (13) that it arguably has replaced "peace, order and good government" as the effective residual clause with respect to selected areas.

More generally, the entire Section 92, entitled "Exclusive Powers of Provincial Governments", is effectively a guarantee that the Canadian federation will be more decentralized than most, since a listing of exclusive sub-national powers does not characterize many federations. For example, the US Constitution articulates a series of federal powers and then leaves all other powers to be assigned to the states or to the citizenry. One rather obvious implication arising from this is that federal heads of power in Canada like "The Regulation of Trade and Commerce" (Section 91 (2)) have been interpreted much more narrowly than is the case for similar provisions in the United States and Australia. Arguably, the reason for this is that neither the Australian High Court nor the United States Supreme Court is faced with the equivalent of a Section 92-type list of exclusive sub-national powers to constrain the sweep of their federal interstate–commerce clauses (as well as a whole host of other federal powers). As a result, some key aspects relating to securing the Canadian internal (cross-border) economic union have to be achieved through the political route rather than through the courts, e.g., the Agreement on Internal Trade (AIT).

There is another, and surely ironic, way in which our Constitution serves to increase the role and the power of the provinces, namely the fact that in terms of our national governing institutions, Canada surely ranks as the world's most centralized federation. Indeed, there is no meaningful provincial representation at all at the centre. This is an extreme version of what in the federalism literature is referred to as "interstate federalism", namely an intergovernmental relationship that has a complete structural separation between the provincial (sub-national) governments and the governing institutions at the centre. The alternative approach, "intrastate federalism", is a structure where the constituent units are brought directly into the operations of the central government. For example, the Canadian Senate resembles the House of Lords in the unitary state the United Kingdom, in that appointments to our Senate are the prerogative of the Prime Minister. In contrast, the traditional second chambers of federal systems represent, in varying ways, the provinces, states, Länder, etc. As important, there is no provincial role in the appointment to national institutions such as the Supreme Court, the Bank of Canada, the Canadian Radio-television and Telecommunications Commission, the Canadian Transport Commission, and on and on. Driven in part by the reality that nature abhors a vacuum, provincial and regional interests have come to be articulated via the provincial premiers, even to the point where, on several occasions, they have become the effective opposition to the federal government of the day.

Given this lack of direct provincial representation at the centre, some other avenues had to be developed to satisfy the joint needs of policy coordination and provincial input. One of the resulting approaches was, and is, "executive federalism": the interchange among the executives of the federal and provincial governments. These federal-provincial dealings run the gamut from informal interchanges among lower-level bureaucrats through to more formal meetings of senior executives and ministers, culminating with first ministers' meetings (FMM). Numbering well in the tens of hundreds, these ongoing federal-provincial meetings, and the concept of executive federalism itself, may well represent Canada's "contribution to the art of federalism" (Safarian 1980: 18). Phrased differently, creative processes have substituted for an inadequate constitutional/institutional structure that, in turn, has led to a more decentralized Canada. The irony here is that a less centralized set of national governing institutions (e.g., a triple-E senate, or a Bundesrat format) would have led to a more centralized federation, or at least one that would have served to diminish the premiers' and provincial governments' roles in the federation.

Two further provisions of the *Constitution Act, 1867* merit highlight in terms of enhancing provincial powers. The first of these is Section 109 ("All Lands, Mines, Minerals and Royalties belonging to the several Provinces ... and all Sums ...payable for such ... shall belong to the several Provinces"). Because of the high variation in provincial endowments of lands, mines, minerals and royalties, this provision would have created interprovincial fiscal balance problems in any event, but more tractable challenges than we now face. The existing horizontal fiscal challenge arose because Ottawa denied the transfer of subsurface rights to Saskatchewan and Alberta when they entered confederation in 1905. When these subsurface rights were returned to the provinces in 1930, the provinces kept these rights and did not transfer them to existing landowners. Not only does this mean that the royalties that accrue directly to these provinces can be (and recently have been) enormous but, as well, they are untaxed by Ottawa by virtue of Section 125 ("No lands or Property belonging to Canada or any Province shall be liable to Taxation."). Similar offshore energy privileges were later granted to Newfoundland and Labrador and to Nova Scotia. Moreover, Ottawa enshrined Section 92A as part of the *Constitution Act, 1982*, a section that further expanded or at least served to reconfirm provincial powers with respect to natural resources. One of the many implications arising from all this has been to wreak havoc with our successive approaches to our equalization program.

The second provision is Section 94 of the *Constitution Act, 1867*, which is an amending formula that allows the common-law provinces (i.e., the non-Quebec provinces) to transfer aspects of "property and civil rights" to Ottawa. That is, it allows the common-law provinces to achieve greater cross-province uniformity in programs that fall under Section 92 (13), essentially social programs. The received wisdom is that Sir John A. Macdonald enshrined this provision in anticipation of a desire by the common-law provinces to achieve a more uniform application of their respective social envelopes. While this clause is deemed to be a 'dead letter' or non-operative, legislation related to the Canada Pension Plan (CPP)/Quebec Pension Plan (QPP) and the 2004 health care agreement fall fully within the spirit of Section 94, as will be elaborated below. In the present context, it serves as a reminder that the 1867 division of powers was deemed by some to be too decentralized for the English-speaking provinces. To the extent that this is indeed the case, one way around this would be to embrace creative instruments and processes which, as will be seen, is precisely what has occurred.

To the above litany, one could add various other provisional aspects of the Constitution, e.g., allowing the provinces to levy direct taxes, which ensures that Canada will be fiscally decentralized. However, the foregoing analysis is sufficient to make the larger point that if other societal pressures are such as to push Canada toward decentralization, then the *Constitution Act, 1867* can be accommodative. And these other centrifugal society forces clearly exist. The combined realities that the two central provinces hold over fifty percent of the population and that the natural trading routes are north-south rather than east-west have, among many other factors, served to enhance the centrifugal forces in the federation.

Some centralizing features

Obviously, there are many unifying features that bind Canadians together. One of these is that despite our linguistic, cultural, legal and geographic diversity, the values that we share and the nature of the country we desire transcend all of the above differences and constitute an important part of the societal glue that attracts all of us to work toward improving the Canadian state and society.

I suspect some of this attraction can be traced to our collective satisfaction with our parliamentary system in comparison to the United States' separation-of-powers approach. Moreover, Canadians are much more comfortable with our Constitutional rhetoric ("Peace, Order and Good Government") than we are with the American constitutional rhetoric ("Life, Liberty and the Pursuit of Happiness"). Arguably, this is the result of the fact that, thanks to our English and French heritages respectively, we have married the Anglo-American economic model with a continental-European version of a social model.

More recently, the Canadian Charter of Rights and Freedoms has become the touchstone of Canadian values and identity for many Canadians, especially in English Canada. One can mount an argument that the Charter is decentralizing or 'Americanizing', that it bestows rights, via the courts, on individuals that Parliament cannot counter and, therefore, leads us to a degree at least down the United States' separation-of-powers road. However, the dominant vision of the Charter is that its "language of rights is a Canadian language not a provincial language" (Cairns 1985), and that "the resultant rights and freedoms [are] country wide in scope, enforced by a national supreme court, and entrenched in a national constitution" (Cairns 1979: 354). The Charter has caught on to such a degree that English-speaking Canadians are beginning to develop a new 'non-territorial' conception of the federation—vested interests versus Charter interests—as it were. At one level, the Charter can be viewed as inimical to Quebec and Quebecers. Specifically, Quebecers may find it hard to accept a concept of Canada where they become 'citizens' by virtue of a set of rights adjudicated by a pan-Canadian Supreme Court and where any Quebec derogations depend on the exercise of the notwithstanding clause which, then, is open to criticism from the rest of Canada. At another level, however, Quebecers can embrace the values and/or freedoms enshrined in the Charter since the Canadian Charter is to a large degree built on the earlier Quebec Charter of Human Rights and Freedoms (*Charte des droits et libertés de la personne*).

Structure versus process

It should be clear from the above analysis that the written constitutional text is not always the final word in terms of the degree to which decentralization (or centralization) characterizes a federation. Rather, creative processes are a necessary complement to the Constitution in ensuring that the federation can respond to either of both changing economic or political forces and the wishes of its citizens. This is, of course, hardly new. Carl Friedrich stated as much forty years ago:

> Federalism should not be seen only as a static pattern or design characterized by a particular and precisely fixed division of powers between government levels. Federalism is also and perhaps primarily the process of ... adopting joint policies and making joint decisions on joint problems (Friedrich 1968: 7).

The good news here is that we Canadians have proven to be masters of this "federalism as process." For example:

- We centralized the Canadian federation during war time and decentralized later without any change in the written constitutional word.
- Changes in the form and magnitude of federal-provincial transfers have been tantamount to formal changes in the distribution of powers, e.g., conditional grants are centralizing and unconditional grants are decentralizing.
- We have found creative ways to generate provincially decentralized, yet nationally harmonized, programs (income taxation, welfare, Medicare...), on which more later.
- We have strategically accommodated asymmetries in key programs across the provinces such as per-

sonal income taxation and the public pension plan. The accepted name for this is 'opting out', although I shall later argue that 'opting in' is a far more appropriate label.

This list could go on, but the above examples will suffice in terms of emphasizing two key process roles. The first is that creative processes enabled provincial programs to embrace pan-Canadian requisites which, in turn, ensured that Canada could continue to benefit from the static and dynamic efficiency associated with decentralized design and delivery. The second is that similarly creative processes allowed Quebec to acquire the trappings of 'nation' within the Canadian state. The purpose of the following section is to elaborate on this point: much of our creative use of process was, and is, driven not so much by a desire for decentralization but rather a desire for each of the *deux nations* concept of Canada.

Centralization/decentralization, asymmetry and *deux nations*

At this juncture, it is necessary to introduce a proposition that is fundamental to understanding the operational dynamics of Canadian federalism. Presumably, there are alternative versions, but the most straightforward version is a slight modification of the one that I entered into evidence as an expert witness before Quebec's Bélanger–Campeau Commission (Courchene 1991).

For Quebecers, Quebec will always be their nation and Canada will always be their state. For the rest of Canadians, Canada tends to be both their nation and their state. Recognizing the different loci for 'nation' for Quebecers and other Canadians will be essential to understanding that much of what Canadians call 'decentralization' is, in reality, the creative exercise of instruments and processes designed to accommodate both 'nations' within the Canadian state.

Relatedly, the inevitable by-product of embracing *deux nations* will be asymmetry. In passing, it should be noted that this separation of nation and state is also an essential component of the identity of our many First Nations and other Aboriginal peoples of Canada. However, attention in what follows is directed only to the Canadian provinces.

Quebec's personal income tax and fiscal decentralization

One of the watershed moments in Canadian political and fiscal federalism was the introduction in 1954 of Quebec's personal income tax (PIT) system. The trigger point for this was Ottawa's 1951 exercise of its spending power by providing grants directly to universities. Quebec (under Duplessis) prohibited its universities from accepting these grants since universities fell under "Property and the Civil Rights" (Section 92 (13)). However, the province quickly realized that it had no access to a revenue source to compensate the universities for this prohibition. This led to Quebec's Royal Commission on Fiscal Relations (The Tremblay Commission), which recommended that the province mount its own PIT, which Quebec did in 1954. The implications of Quebec's PIT were dramatic and wide-ranging:

- Ottawa responded by creating the Tax Sharing Arrangements (1957), which gave all provinces the choice of levying their own taxes or receiving an abatement of federal tax. All of the non-Quebec provinces opted for the abatement which was allocated on a derivation principle (i.e., on the basis of what was actually collected in each province).
- The impact of these derivation-based abatements was to generate different amounts of per capita revenues across provinces. To ameliorate these per capita differences, Ottawa introduced Canada's formal equalization program in the same year. Without an equalization program, the poorer provinces would not have allowed the ensuing significant PIT decen-

tralization to occur. Nor, therefore, would the rich provinces have been able to enjoy the fruits of their above-national-average tax bases.

- As Claude Forget (1984: 194) noted, in the years before 1954, the programs relating to unemployment, old age pensions and family allowances were established with federal financing, regulation and administration. The first two required constitutional amendments, and all three were in areas of provincial jurisdiction. However, "after 1954 came even more significant spending programs: hospital insurance; Medicare; and social assistance. All of these later programs were to be cost-shared with the provinces, but provincially administered."

Arguably, therefore, this post-1954 shift from federally-funded, federally-regulated and federally-administered programs to shared-cost programs under provincial design and administration is also part of the legacy of the Quebec PIT, and ultimately of the unwanted (by Quebec) exercise of the federal spending power in areas of provincial jurisdiction.

There is no question that this overall episode paved the way for a significant increase in both fiscal and social policy decentralization. In particular, as the provincial role in implementing Canada's social envelope increased, so did the transfer of PIT tax points to the provinces. Over time, the shared-PIT system (Ottawa and Canada outside of Quebec) underwent changes that ensured the provinces would not fragment the economic union, with the result that this shared-PIT system became a model for a decentralized federal system—decentralized, yet highly harmonized.

This will be a hallmark of much of the following analysis, namely the creative ways in which our federation can combine harmonization with decentralization. The example of the nine non-Quebec provinces piggy-backing on the federal PIT system has been carried over to many other areas, as the next section illustrates.

National programs, 'opting in' and Section 94

In terms of the personal income tax model alluded to above, Quebec had its own separate PIT while the remaining provinces chose to link themselves with the federal system that required them to accept certain federally-determined variables such as the definition of income. Should any province wish, however, it can follow Quebec's lead and establish its own separate PIT since the provinces have a right to direct taxation by virtue of Section 92 (2). In effect, this is *de jure* symmetry but *de facto* asymmetry.

Intriguingly, however, virtually all analysts would refer to Quebec's establishing its own personal income tax system as 'opting out' by Quebec. But having one's own PIT system is a provincial right. How can one be 'opting out' by running one's own PIT, when it is your constitutional right to do so. The reality is that the other nine provinces are foregoing their right to establish their own personal income tax systems, i.e., the provinces other than Quebec are 'opting in' to the overarching federal program.

This pattern has been repeated across a wide range of programs, some of which are detailed below. By way of an overview of what follows, the following observations are in order:

- The dual PIT regime is a *deux nations* solution. Quebec's PIT is an integral component of its interpretation of "property and civil rights". And the remaining nine provinces have decided to come together with a common approach that links them closely with the federal PIT system. This is consistent with the earlier proposition that the non-Quebec provinces associate 'nation' with Ottawa. Therefore, the PIT arrangements meet the 'national' criteria for all provinces.
- Moreover, this is also fully consistent with Section 94, which, as noted, provides a constitutional way for the rest of Canada outside of Quebec to transfer aspects of "property and civil rights" to Ottawa and, in the process, to make these programs more uniform across all common-law provinces.

Among the initiatives that are variations on this theme are the following:

- In the *Constitution Act, 1964*, the powers with respect to contributory public pensions were enshrined in a manner that made them concurrent with provincial paramountcy. This allowed Canada to enact the Canada Pension Plan for the nine common-law provinces and it also allowed Quebec to exercise its paramountcy and establish the Quebec Pension Plan. Again, the 'national' nature of the pension plans was achieved. And again, the general view that Quebec has 'opted out' because it exercised its constitutional right seems to be much less accurate than the assertion that the common-law provinces have 'opted in' because they waived their paramount right to establish their own programs. One should add, however, that the CPP and the QPP remain very similar in terms of their operating parameters. The major difference—that Quebec invested its surplus QPP funds in capital markets whereas the CPP invested its surplus funds in provincial bonds—has recently been eliminated with the CPP establishing an arm's length investment fund.
- At the July 2004 meeting of the Council of the Federation, the provinces agreed to a proposal that would transfer responsibility for Pharmacare to the federal government. As part of this proposal there was unanimous provincial agreement that Quebec would maintain its own program and receive comparable compensation from Ottawa. Not only does this address the *deux nations* approach to national programs, but it also is rather clear that the nine provinces are 'opting in' to a federally-run scheme rather than Quebec 'opting out'. Indeed, since this would be a transfer by the nine provinces other than Quebec of provincial powers to Ottawa, this is precisely the case envisioned by Section 94.

- While then Prime Minister Paul Martin did not embrace the provincial Pharmacare proposal at the September 2004 First Ministers' Meeting, Ottawa and the provinces did sign an historic 10-year, C$ 41 billion Medicare agreement. An integral part of the agreement was an 'asymmetric federalism' rider, jointly signed by Ottawa and Quebec (Canada 2004) to the effect that Quebec's policies under this agreement "would be determined in accordance with the objectives, standards, and criteria established by the relevant Quebec authorities". Again, a variation of the *deux nations* thesis.
- Finally the on-going attempt to create a pan-Canadian Securities Commission may also fall into the *deux nations* category. Since securities regulation has traditionally been a provincial power falling under Section 92 (13), Quebec will maintain its own securities commission. The remaining provinces may well 'opt in' to a federally run commission.

These, and other examples, confirm Sir John A. Macdonald's expectation that over the years, the common-law provinces would wish to pursue a more uniform approach to selected policy areas that fall under "property and civil rights". Although Section 94 has never been formally utilized, the spirit of Section 94 has been alive and well and is arguably becoming ever more relevant.

Why this much emphasis on 'opting out' versus 'opting in'?

One part of the answer is that it is important to label things correctly. In particular, the terminology employed will influence the way in which the federation comes to view itself. An emphasis on Quebec's continual 'opting out' and creating asymmetric arrangements leads Canadians rather naturally to refer to this as excessive decentralization. But suppose we spoke in terms of the common-law provinces abandoning their constitutional prerogatives and linking with Ottawa to create more uniform social programs. Then the focus would be on the initiatives by the nine common-law provinces to make social programs more uniform and, therefore, serving to centralize key aspects of the federation. In my view, had we adopted this latter vision, the result would not only be a more accurate representation of the underlying reality, but it would also go a long way toward creating a more accommodative place for Quebec in the federation, in comparison to the *status quo* which incorrectly and unfairly associates Quebec with asymmetrical 'opting out' and with the post-war decentralization of the federation.

Making decentralized provincial programs pan-Canadian: a model for decentralized federations

To this point, too much emphasis has been directed toward how we currently view our social programs at the expense of understanding the manner in which the post-war underdeveloped provincial programs were converted into well-funded and effective pan-Canadian programs. The time frame for creating social Canada was from the mid-to-late 1950s through to the 1963–68 Pearson era.

At the heart of the strategy were four important features. The first was the introduction of conditional fifty percent shared-cost grants for hospital insurance, Medicare, postsecondary education and welfare. The second was the creation of the equalization program in 1957 and its progressive broadening and deepening, so that all provinces had access to reasonably comparable per capita revenues at reasonably comparable tax rates. The third was the transfer of tax points to enrich the coffers of the provinces (which helped finance the growth of the social programs). Finally, in connection with the earlier-mentioned shared-cost programs, Ottawa introduced a series of measures (no residence requirements for accessing these programs, comprehensive coverage, no discrimination, etc.) that served to link these provincial programs into versions of pan-Canadian systems.

In one sense, this represented a massive exercise of the federal spending power in areas of exclusive provincial jurisdiction. In another sense, however, it represented the creation of a set of processes and instrumentalities that

allowed Canadians to have access to comparable social programs wherever they might reside or move to, all the while
preserving and strengthening the ability of the provinces
to maintain their decentralized design, administration and
delivery of these programs.

Later, as these programs became established and cher-
ished by all Canadians, Ottawa was able to convert the
cost-sharing into block-funding and to remove most of the
regulatory conditionality. The key point to note is that the
current provincial control of the social envelope was made
possible initially by a significant financial and regulatory
intrusion by Ottawa into provincial jurisdiction. Therefore, while we may refer to the social envelope as being
decentralized, one should recognize the very important
role that Ottawa played not only in enriching these programs in the first place but, as well, in linking the various
provincial programs into pan-Canadian regimes. Phrased
differently, the exercise of the federal spending power in
areas of exclusive provincial jurisdiction served in the case
of our social programs to entrench the decentralization of
these programs.

Suppose that we were unable to accommodate Quebec
and the rest of Canada in their desire to create 'national'
programs and policies. Rather than the current arrangements, there would be some intermediate result that
would leave both communities wanting. From the van-
tage point of the two sides, this would be an inferior solution, one that would clearly reduce welfare. It seems clear,
therefore, that approaches which allow both Quebec and
the rest of Canada to achieve what they perceive as superior solutions are to be celebrated. The issue of whether
the resulting solutions are centralizing or decentralizing
is quite beside the point: they are welfare-enhancing for
all Canadians! Moreover, they are efficiency-enhancing as
well, in the sense of the analysis in the second section of
this paper above.

In any event, on November 27, 2007, the House of Commons unanimously proclaimed that "the Québécois form a
nation within a united Canada."

Asymmetry and deux nations

As already noted, asymmetry is the inevitable by-product of implementing a *deux nations* strategy. Nonetheless, I think that it is fair to say most Canadians would view the resulting asymmetry as being caused by Quebec's 'opting out'. But why should the asymmetry that results because the nine common-law provinces opt to piggy-back on to the federal personal income tax system be laid at the feet of Quebec? And prospectively, should the rest of Canada join with Ottawa in establishing an overarching securities regulator, why should the asymmetry arising from a decision by Quebec to maintain its securities commission be viewed as the trigger for the asymmetry? Therefore, just as the earlier analysis relating to 'opting in' and 'opting out' argued that associating Quebec with 'opting out' is uncalled for and politically detrimental, likewise associating asymmetry with actions by Quebec must be rethought.

My preference would be to think of asymmetry not in terms of centralization or decentralization and not as a problem but, rather, as a solution that allows Quebec and the rest of Canada to advance along their journey of nation building.

However, I recognize that some analysts are concerned that excessive asymmetry could lead to what the British call the 'West Lothian problem', i.e., should Scottish MPs be able to vote in the House of Commons on those policy areas where they have opted out to mount their own programs? In the Canadian context, the issue would be that if the nine common-law provinces opt to work with Ottawa in several areas, should Quebec MPs still be able to vote on measures relating to these areas, when Quebec will not be bound by the measures, since the province is running its own version of the programs? Assuming that Quebec MPs would even want to vote on issues where this came up, my answer in most if not all cases would be yes.

Consider the recapitalization of the CPP, orchestrated by then Finance Minister Paul Martin, that raised the CPP contribution rate to 9.9 percent. Quebec agreed to go along with the premium increase in the QPP as well, so there was no reason for the province's MPs not to exercise their vote in the House of Commons should they so wish. I think that this "West Lothian" issue is yet another area where applying the equivalent of the 'opting out' rhetoric can lead to inappropriate conclusions. Specifically, should foregoing the right to mount their own programs and linking up with the federal program serve to increase the House of Commons' role of the nine common-law provinces' MPs relative to Quebec MPs, or MPs of provinces that have chosen to mount their own programs? Phrased this way, the answer is more clearly a 'no'. Therefore, my recommendation to one and all is to recognize that asymmetry is a (probably inelegant) solution rather than a problem. Were the unlikely to occur, and asymmetry began to pervade the system, then let's cross that bridge when we come to it.

Is decentralization endogeneous?

In light of the above analysis, it is appropriate to raise the issue of whether decentralization (or centralization) is an independent driver with its own internal dynamic or whether it can better be viewed as an accommodative instrument responding to deeper societal values and forces.

Readers will recognize that the case for decentralization as an endogenous instrumentality has been a recurring theme thus far in this essay. Beyond the written constitutional word, provincial powers were further enhanced: a) because the Constitution lacked a role for the provinces in the central governing institutions; b) because judicial review ended up interpreting the Constitution in ways that effectively assigned additional responsibilities to the provinces; c) because creative processes and protocols were developed to ensure that programs delivered at the provincial level could become pan-Canadian; and d) because the evolution of asymmetric arrangements for a variety of programs and policy areas (taxation, health care, aspects of employment insurance, and soon perhaps securities regulation and Pharmacare) is being driven by the reality that Quebec and the rest of Canada have a different jurisdictional locus for 'nation'.

In all of these areas, it is arguably more correct to maintain that decentralization and asymmetry have emerged not as drivers but rather as key instruments or by-products in the process of accommodating the underlying reality that our federation itself is in many dimensions diverse and multi-national.

This can, of course, be a two-way street. With the advent of the new global order, many of the policy areas that are emerging as the key to success in this new environment (human capital development, cities, etc.) fall into a category that elsewhere (Courchene 2008) I have labelled NI/PJ, i.e., in the national interest but under provincial jurisdiction. Strict adherence to 'open federalism', *à la* Prime Minister Harper, may well satisfy Quebec, but this 21st century version of 'watertight compartments' will, almost by definition, fall short of the needs and desires of the other provinces.

If one assumes, as I do, that Ottawa will have to assign priority to these areas, then the issue becomes one of instrument choice. One possibility would be to follow the spirit of the earlier-noted Pharmacare proposal: the nine provinces joining with Ottawa, and Quebec running its own program with comparable federal compensation. Another would be an approach that followed the 2004 health care format, replete with a Canada–Quebec asymmetric rider. In both these cases, the result embodies some centralization (for the nine provinces), some decentralization (for Quebec) and therefore some asymmetry. If the past is any guide, our societal preference would be to view this as 'opting out' by Quebec, resulting in asymmetry and decentralization. As is clear from the above analysis, my preference would be to refer to this as 'opting in' by the rest of Canada. The key point is that the driving force here is the exogenous challenge thrown up by the new global order, and the instrument chosen to address this challenge should be viewed as an endogenous response. The fact that the response will likely reflect the underlying characteristics and values of our federation should not be surprising.

This can be put in an international comparative perspective in terms of federal systems. Consider four federations: Australia, Germany, Canada and the United States. Australia is not only the most centralized of the four, but it is also a highly egalitarian nation. Welfare payments are centralized; university wage grids are national; sheep and wine are features of all states and territories; per capita income differences across states are much narrower than in Canada; and so on. Australia also has the most comprehensive and egalitarian equalization program: transfers to the states are equalized upwards and downwards for both revenue means and expenditure needs. Hence the most egalitarian of the four federations has the most egalitarian and centralized system of political and fiscal intergovernmental relations.

Germany is the second most-uniform federation of our chosen sample. Tax rates for all major taxes are set nationally. Most legislation affecting the Länder is enacted federally, although implementation of this legislation falls to the Länder. The German equalization system is also very comprehensive, including an inter-Länder revenue sharing system. Underlying this high degree of redistribution is the imperative in the German Basic Law (the constitution) for 'uniformity of living conditions'. Hence, the second most egalitarian federation has the second most equalizing set of fiscal transfers.

As the above analysis has emphasized *en passant*, Canada is among the most decentralized federation in terms of sub-national revenues and expenditures, of linguistic and legal dualism, and so on. Not surprisingly, Canada's system of intergovernmental transfers reflects the diverse and decentralized nature of our federation. Moreover, welfare is provincial and the benefit rates vary considerably across the provinces. Likewise, not surprisingly, our equalization is not as egalitarian as that in Australia or Germany, since we equalize only on the revenue side and, even then, the equalization is only partial in that we do not equalize the rich provinces downward.

What is unique about the United States is that it is the only federation that does not have a formal revenue-equalization program. Presumably, part of the rationale for this is that any revenue-raising-capacity differences across states will be capitalized in wages, rents and property values, so that there is nothing left to equalize, as it were: low-revenue states have correspondingly lower costs for delivering public services. This accords with the "rugged individualism" that is at the heart of the American creed. Obviously, it also correlates well with the American constitutional rhetoric, "Life, Liberty and the Pursuit of Happiness".

What is clear from all this is that intergovernmental arrangements and national/sub-national relationships across federations are anything but arbitrary. Indeed, they complement the tax and expenditure assignments in ways that integrate overall fiscal federalism in directions consistent with the implicit or explicit norms and values of their respective federations and societies. And it is precisely because these intergovernmental transfers are so embedded in the value systems of their societies that their distinctive features are not portable across federations. Phrased differently, describing aspects of their intergovernmental relations and transfers is tantamount to describing key aspects of the societal value systems.

In this sense, Canadian decentralization is endogenous in that it resonates well with the underlying nature and values of Canadian society. We would wreak havoc with all that is near and dear to us if we were to import the Australian intergovernmental regime, let alone the American approach. And Australia could likewise not countenance Canada's socio-economic and fiscal arrangements.

Conclusion

Geography, legal and linguistic dualism, cultural pluralism, the east-west variability of our north-south integration...and of course our Constitutional division of powers dictated that Canada must be a decentralized federation. Over the years, we Canadians invoked creative processes (e.g., executive federalism) and bridging instrumentalities (e.g., the Council of the Federation) to ensure that we were able to combine the static and dynamic efficiencies associated with decentralized design and delivery with the traditional unitary-state advantages of overarching national programs. Moreover, those same efforts with equally creative structures and processes were at play in the accommodation of Quebec's specificity within the Canadian political family, and culminated with the unanimous parliamentary proclamation that "the Québécois form a nation within a united Canada". We are well on our way to ensuring that our Aboriginal peoples can likewise achieve nation status within the Canadian framework.

While there are many factors and forces that have played key roles in the evolution of our federation, one of the most impressive features has been our ability to work together to align our decentralized federation—sometimes centralizing, sometimes decentralizing a bit more—in ways that build on our underlying values and norms in our collective exercise at nation building.

Endnote

[1] It is a pleasure to acknowledge the helpful comments from Nadia Verrelli.

References

Cairns, Alan 1979. "Recent Federalist Constitutional Proposals: A Review Essay." *Canadian Public Policy*, 5: 348–365.

Cairns, Alan 1985. "The Politics of Constitution Making: The Canadian Experience." In *Redesigning the State: Constitutional Change in Historical Perspective*, eds. K. Banting and R. Simeon. Toronto: University of Toronto Press, 95–145.

Canada 2004. Canadian Intergovernmental Conference Secretariat. *Asymmetrical Federalism that Respects Quebec's Jurisdiction* [on-line] http://www.scics.gc.ca/cinfo04/800042012_e.pdf [consulted March 26, 2010].

Courchene, Thomas J. 1991. Expert witness (presentations and testimony) before *La commission sur l'avenir politique et constitutionnel du Québec*

(Bélanger–Campeau Commission), *Quebec Hansard*. January 15, no. 25, 1896–1907. A version of this appears as *The Community of the Canadas*. Réflexions/Reflections no. 8. Kingston, ON: Queen's University, Institute of Intergovernmental Relations.

Courchene, Thomas J. 2001. *A State of Minds: Toward a Human Capital Future for Canadians*. Montreal: Institute for Research on Public Policy.

Courchene, Thomas J. 2006 (September). "Variations on the Federalism Theme." *Policy Options*, 46–54.

Courchene, Thomas J. 2007. *Global Future for Canada's Global Cities*. (Policy Matters Series, 8: 2). Montreal: Institute for Research on Public Policy.

Courchene, Thomas J. 2008 (Fall) "Reflections on the Federal Spending Power: Practice, Principles and Perspectives." *Queen's Law Journal*, 34: 1: 75–124.

Fleiner, Thomas 2010. "Different Constitutional Underpinnings of Federalism: Common vs Continental Civil Law." In *The Federal Idea: Federalism*, eds. Thomas J. Courchene et al. Kingston, ON: Queen's University, Institute of Intergovernmental Relations and McGill-Queen's University Press.

Forget, Claude 1984. "Quebec's Experience with the Personal Income Tax." In *A Separate Personal Income Tax for Ontario: Background Studies*, ed. David Conklin. Toronto: Ontario Economic Council, 187–212.

Friedman, Thomas 1999. *The Lexus and the Olive Tree: Understanding Globalization*. New York: Farrar, Strauss and Giroux.

Friedrich, Carl 1968. *Trends of Federalism in Theory and Practice*. New York: Praeger.

Harrison, Kathryn, ed. 2006. *Racing to the Bottom: Provincial Interdependence in the Canadian Federation*. Vancouver: University of British Columbia Press.

McKinnon, Ronald 1997. "Monetary Regimes, Government Borrowing Constraints, and Market-Preserving Federalism: Implications for EMU." In *The Nation State in a Global/Information Era: Policy Challenges*, ed. Thomas J. Courchene. Kingston, ON: Queen's University, John Deutsch Institute for the Study of Economic and Financial Policy, 1001–1141.

Oates, Wallace 1972. *Fiscal Federalism*. New York: Harcourt, Brace, Jovanovich, Inc.

Safarian, A.E. 1980. *Ten Markets or One? Regional Barriers to Economic Activity*. Toronto: Ontario Economic Council.

Weingast, Barry 1995. "The Economic Role of Political Institutions: Market Preserving Federalism and Economic Developments." *Journal of Law and Economics and Organization*, 11: 1–31.

Chapter 2

The Practical Defence of Decentralization

Ian Peach

Introduction

I am not a dyed-in-the-wool, ideological decentralizer. Indeed, as the son of a career federal civil servant, the idea that national politics and a federal role in making national policy matters could be said to be bred in the bone. I am also, however, someone who has spent most of his career in the service of provincial and territorial governments, either working on intergovernmental affairs directly or working on issues with important intergovernmental dimensions. Thus, my career has exposed me to the perverse effects on policy making of a federal government that does not understand its appropriate role and insists on inserting itself into a public policy problem without an adequate commitment to engaging provinces and territories in joint problem-solving. While this background leads me to prefer intergovernmental cooperation in addressing national problems, in the absence of a federal commitment to using its policy tools carefully, and thus more effectively, I can only conclude that the 'evil' of decentralization is by far the lesser, compared to the 'evil' of federal unilateralism.

Nonetheless, I still hold out hope for federalism and for intergovernmental relations. There is still value in having a federal government play a role in making public policy in Canada, as long as the extent and limit of that role is prop-

erly understood and respected. This chapter will review
both the case for a federal role and the case for limitations
on that role. It will also review when and how the federal
government could better exercise its powers to contribute
more effectively to solving public policy problems. Lastly, it
will discuss balancing the decentralization of authority in a
manner more consistent with the constitutional division of
powers, with strong norms of intergovernmental coordination, through the more effective of the mechanisms of
intergovernmental decision making. This can be more effective in addressing national policy problems than the federal
unilateralism and 'direction setting' on which we have come
to rely too much. While this prescription will be decentralist, it will be what one might call an argument for a 'federalist's decentralization'.[1]

Taming the beast: previous efforts at constraining the federal role in national policy making

The desire to constrain the federal government's role is by
no means new. Limiting federal authority to act in areas
assigned by the Constitution to the provinces, through
the limitation of the federal spending power, has been an
issue on Quebec's political agenda since even before the
Quiet Revolution. Beginning with the Victoria Charter
in 1971, each time Canadian governments sought agreement to amend the Constitution, proposals to limit the
federal government's ability to act unilaterally through the
spending power were part of the agenda (Smiley 1983: 75;
Constitutional Accord 1987, section 7; Consensus Report
on the Constitution August 28, 1992: paragraph 25).

While these proposals were originally spearheaded by
Quebec, other provinces also came to support the limitation
of the federal spending power over the years, as they became
concerned about the perverse effects on provincial policy decisions of federal intervention. By the time of the negotiations
toward the Charlottetown Accord in 1992, provinces, led by

Ontario, had also come to realize that federal interventions in areas of provincial jurisdiction through the spending power created a second risk: of unilateral federal withdrawal of support for programs on which citizens had come to depend, thereby leaving provinces with additional fiscal pressures. This was the story of the unilateral federal imposition of a cap on transfers to provinces under the Canada Assistance Plan (the "cap on CAP" problem) and the provinces' subsequent loss in the Supreme Court of Canada of their legal challenge to the unilateral federal withdrawal (Canada Assistance Plan (BC) 2.S.C.R. 525). Thus, the Charlottetown Accord text reflects a two-pronged approach to limiting the federal spending power: by limiting new federal exercises of its spending power; and unilateral withdrawal of federal spending where it exists (Consensus Report on the Constitution August 28, 1992 Part III). Both of these efforts were linked by recognition of the damaging effects to provincial policy and fiscal stability that unilateral federal interventions create.

With the defeat of the Charlottetown Accord in 1992, efforts at major, national constitutional reform ceased for the time being, but federal unilateralism and efforts to constrain it certainly did not. In its 1995 budget, the Chrétien government severely cut transfer payments for health care, social services and post-secondary education, leaving provinces and territories in the position of having to assume a far greater proportion of the spending needed in these areas to meet the demands of citizens, at the same time as they were wrestling with crippling budgetary deficits themselves (Facal 2005).

As this was also the period immediately before and after the 1995 Quebec referendum on sovereignty, provinces and territories sought to wrest the role of leadership in social policy reform away from the federal government by demonstrating that provinces and territories, acting in concert, could be at least as effective at creating national policy as the federal government. As Facal has noted, this concern grew as the federal government's fiscal situation stabilized and it began to initiate new programs in areas of provincial jurisdiction through direct transfers to individuals and institutions (Ibid.).

These efforts were coordinated by the provincial/territorial Ministerial Council on Social Policy Renewal, which was established by Premiers in 1996, and the subsequently established federal/provincial/territorial Ministerial Council (Warriner and Peach 2007: 72). Their efforts to make social policy through intergovernmental coordination included an effort aimed directly at constraining the federal spending power through the Social Union Framework agreement (SUFA). At one point in the negotiation of the SUFA, provinces and territories accomplished the remarkable achievement of securing the consensus of all provinces and territories, including Quebec, on a proposed outline for the agreement. This "Saskatoon Consensus" (so named because the Annual Premiers Conference of 1998, at which Quebec agreed to participate in the SUFA negotiations, took place in Saskatoon) represented the first time that the Quebec government had participated in multilateral discussions of social policy and the use of the federal spending power since the Charlottetown Accord had failed (Warriner and Peach 2007: 145, 147). From Quebec's perspective, it also represented the first time in this period that all of the other provinces and territories were prepared to agree to the traditional Quebec demand for full compensation for provinces that opted out of a new national program (Facal 2005: 2). The relevant text of the Saskatoon communiqué read:

> Premiers emphasized that the flexibility afforded to provinces/territories through the ability to opt out of any new or modified Canada-wide social programs in areas of provincial/territorial jurisdiction with full compensation, provided that the province/territory carries on a program that addresses the priority of the Canada-wide program, is an essential dimension of the provincial/territorial consensus negotiating position (Canada 1998).

Unfortunately, this consensus did not last. While the position contained in the Saskatoon Consensus was affirmed by all provinces and territories in Victoria, British Columbia on January 29, 1999, unofficial negotiations with the federal government occurred in the subsequent days (Facal 2005: 3). The federal government, in exchange for an offer of additional funds for health care, secured concessions from the provinces and territories other than Quebec on the Saskatoon Consensus, the most important of which was on the opting out provision (Warriner and Peach 2007: 153). As a result, Quebec refused to agree to the Social Union Framework Agreement that was signed on February 4, 1999.

While other premiers agreed to the Social Union Framework Agreement, some did so reluctantly and with some degree of suspicion about the federal government's commitment to abide by its terms. As it turned out, there was some basis for this suspicion: not long after the signing of the SUFA, the federal government launched its Homelessness Initiative, a new national program that was, essentially, fully formed in Ottawa and had not been the subject of intergovernmental discussion prior to its launch. Federal actions such as the launch of the Homelessness Initiative and its reluctance to establish an intergovernmental body to resolve disputes over the interpretation of the *Canada Health Act*, which had been committed to by all signatories to the SUFA, led to the agreement's quickly diminished authority and relevance to intergovernmental relations in Canada. While it is still 'on the books' as an intergovernmental agreement, it is generally acknowledged to have been a failure (Robson and Schwanen 1999).

The frustration over the inability of provinces and territories to prevent federal intrusion into areas of provincial jurisdiction through the limitation of the federal spending power in part led provincial and territorial governments, in the first half of the present decade, to seek to limit the federal government's fiscal capacity so that the exercise of its spending power would be impractical. Again, as with the efforts to limit the federal spending power, efforts to correct the 'vertical fiscal imbalance' that, it was argued, led to large federal budgetary surpluses was spearheaded by Quebec, though the Quebec government had allies in a number of other provinces. The essence of the Quebec argument is that the division of tax resources between the federal and provincial orders of government is not proportional to the division of expenditure responsibilities between them (Facal 2005: 14). This situation creates an opportunity for the federal government to use its excess fiscal capacity to make policy in areas of provincial jurisdiction.

The Harper government, in its first term, committed to solving the fiscal imbalance: with the current economic crisis and the anticipated federal deficits that will be a consequence of its economic stimulus plan, one could reasonably claim that the fiscal imbalance has been solved. On the other hand, with no meaningful guarantees that future federal governments will exercise restraint and act through intergovernmental mechanisms, a robust economy and increased federal tax revenues could see a return of the fiscal imbalance, federal unilateralism and intergovernmental conflict.

The importance of knowing what you don't know: subsidiarity and the value of local knowledge as an argument for decentralization

One must ask why the issue of limiting federal unilateral action in areas of provincial jurisdiction has had such staying power on the intergovernmental agenda. The obvious answer is that the exercise of federal authority in areas that the Constitution assigns to provinces, when uninvited by provinces or subject to provincial concurrence, offends a variety of rationales for having a federal system in Canada in the first place.

One classically liberal articulation of the purpose for having a federal state can be traced back to Madison's "Federalist No. 51". In Madison's theory, federalism helps to secure liberal freedoms by dividing power between different orders of government, representing different groups, thereby preventing any single ruler or majority from exercising complete power in a despotic fashion (Madison 1788). Clearly, if a federal government can use its fiscal capacity and spending authority to act in any area of jurisdiction according to its own interests, it can undermine this purpose of federalism, by securing to itself a substantial, if not complete, scope of authority to act despotically.

A second purpose of federalism is of greater relevance to Canada: by providing distinct, pre-existing political communities (and in the case of Quebec, a distinct linguistic, cultural and legal community), the exclusive authority to act in areas that are important to securing the continuing distinctiveness of those communities, federalism provides an important support and protection to the multinational character of the Canadian political community. It is clear from the debates at the conferences that preceded Confederation in 1867 that this was a central purpose of establishing Canada as a federal state. Sir George-Etienne Cartier provided a cogent articulation of this point in the Canadian Legislative Assembly in 1865. He stated:

> What was the best and most practicable mode of bringing the provinces together so that particular rights and interests should be properly guarded and protected? No other scheme presented itself but the federation system, and that was the project which now recommended itself to the parliament of Canada. Some parties ... pretended that it was impossible to carry out federation, on account of the differences of races and religions. Those who took this view of the question were in error. It was just the reverse. It was precisely on account of the variety of races, local interests, etc., that the federation system ought to be resorted to and would be found to work well (quoted in Ajzenstat 2003: 285).

If a federal government is able to use its spending power to intervene in these areas and replace provincial policy choices in areas of provincial jurisdiction with its policy choices, it risks undermining policy choices that have been designed to protect the distinctiveness of sub-state communities. This has been the core of Quebec's opposition to the unilateral use of the federal spending power to centralize policy making in Canada. As Kennett has observed, the case for national principles or standards is in dynamic tension with the values of diversity and pluralism that provide the basic rational for federal, rather than unitary, government in Canada and this cannot simply be glossed over by supporters of centralization and national standards (Kennett 1998).

It is a third rationale for federalism, however, that I wish to focus on, as experience suggests that the practical problems with unilateral federal policy making in areas of provincial jurisdiction simply serve to reinforce the value of this principle.

At heart, my argument for decentralization is an argument for governing more intelligently, and therefore effectively, by being honest about where the knowledge necessary to respond to public policy problems effectively lies. The principle that guides this approach to federalism is subsidiarity. Commonly used in debates about the allocation of authority within the European Union but rarely discussed in Canada, the principle of subsidiarity states that governmental authority should be exercised by the smallest, most local unit of government that is capable of exercising that authority effectively; authority should also only be exercised by a larger unit of government to the extent necessary to achieve its objectives (Hueglin 2007).

Subsidiarity shows a preference for local decision making because of the value of local knowledge in understanding and defining a problem, the responsiveness of governments that are close to a problem and therefore have a more direct and clear understanding of the problem, and the degree of creativity that can be applied to solving a problem when those who share in the lived reality of that problem work together to create solutions.

As well, local experimentation in attempting to solve social problems has a lower cost than do a large, national-scale experiments, so smaller units of government should have a higher tolerance for the risk inherent in experimentation. This would be especially true if the costs of failed experiments could be dispersed, through financial support from the federal government, in recognition of the value to society as a whole of encouraging local experimentation.

I can attest to the fact that the importance of local knowledge, and the refined understanding of both a problem and its political salience that comes from that knowledge, cannot be stressed enough. Public policy problems, even if they are common to a number of political communities, manifest themselves differently in different environments. As such, the most effective solution to a problem may well vary depending on local circumstances. As well, the importance of an issue will vary depending on the local circumstances, such as how large a proportion of the community is affected by a problem and whether other problems are of greater concern to the community.

In a country as large and diverse as Canada, not to mention one as culturally, politically and legalistically pluralist, imagining that a single, national program will provide the most effective solution to any problem that requires the active intervention of public officials seems hopelessly naive. Far more common in Canada is the circumstance in which federal insistence on applying a national 'solution' to all manifestations of a problem throughout the country serves to impede progress, create intergovernmental tension, and undermine the capacity and effectiveness of those closest to a public policy problem in addressing that problem. The federal government's inability to demonstrate substantive results from these sorts of interventions merely serves to demonstrate the value of paying proper attention to the principle of subsidiarity.

Some examples from my personal experience in intergovernmental relations may make this point more tangible. Earlier, I mentioned the federal Homelessness Initiative. Saskatchewan, where I worked from 1995 to 2007, does not have a significant problem with absolute homelessness, with people living and sleeping on its streets. This is the logical consequence of a practical reality of life in Saskatchewan; the province gets sufficiently cold for a sufficiently long period of time in the winter that those who are absolutely homeless are likely to succumb each winter. This, however, does not mean that Saskatchewan does not have a homelessness problem; rather, homelessness in Saskatchewan normally manifests itself in the phenomenon of 'couch surfing,' in which individuals move frequently from location to location, seeking a place to sleep each night from shelters or friends (or those who wish to exploit their vulnerability). While these homeless people have shelter and cannot be seen on the streets, they are no less homeless than the 'absolutely homeless'. Their lives are just as uncertain, they are just as vulnerable to predators because of their marginalization and, often related problems, and they have the same problems with securing an education or employment because of their instability.

Yet the federal Homelessness Initiative, because it was designed by officials in Ottawa to address the problem of people living on the streets (which is what homelessness means in the cities they know best), was originally inapplicable in Saskatchewan; it was only expanded to take account of the form of homelessness that exists in Saskatchewan after significant lobbying by senior provincial government officials. If the design of a response to the problem of homelessness had begun at the level of local or provincial/territorial governments, the resources expended by the federal government in designing a program that subsequently had to be redesigned and those expended by the provincial government in lobbying the federal government to make these changes could have been expended, instead, on actually addressing the needs of the homeless.

Similarly, when I was involved in the attempt to negotiate a First Nations self-government agreement between the Federation of Saskatchewan Indian Nations (FSIN), the Government of Canada, and the Government of Saskatchewan, those of us who lived together in Saskatchewan, and approached these negotiations with an understanding of the issues that confronted First Nations people in the province, regularly confronted a federal government that was intransigent in its refusal to adapt an excessively detailed 'negotiation' mandate that had been established to govern the course of all self-government negotiations across Canada to the realities of the situation that existed in Saskatchewan. This made action on the interest of the other two parties to the negotiation impossible in attempting some innovative solutions that had the possibility, at least, of addressing the key issues on the negotiating agenda. This is an approach to negotiation that could be, and on occasion was, described as negotiation in name only.

One example of such a confrontation was the proposal jointly put forward by the negotiators for the provincial government and the FSIN to negotiate a socio-economic strategy, and a socio-economic fund to support the strategy, to be implemented in conjunction with the self-government agreement. The argument, in essence, was that, without improvements to the socio-economic circumstances of First Nations people in Saskatchewan, self-government would be "the administration of misery", in the words of one of the negotiators for the FSIN. Having recognized the importance of addressing the socio-economic circumstances of Aboriginal people in the province along with self-government and the implementation of Aboriginal rights, the provincial government had already made significant new investments in initiatives designed to improve the socio-economic circumstance of Aboriginal peoples and was prepared to make these investments part of the intergovernmental strategy. In other words, the province was prepared to take a risk on a major new initiative because it recognized the importance both of rectifying the socio-economic disadvantages of First Nations people in the province and of doing so in cooperation with First Nations themselves.

The federal government, however, refused to negotiate a socio-economic strategy in conjunction with the self-government negotiations, as the federal officials did not have a mandate to do so. In fact, the federal officials involved in these self-government negotiations attempted to secure approval for a change of mandate to allow them to undertake both negotiations simultaneously, but they met with resistance within the federal bureaucracy; other federal officials explained, on one occasion at the negotiation table, that such an approach could not be agreed to, as it might "set a precedent". To his credit, one of the senior federal negotiators pointed out that setting a precedent for doing something that worked was not a negative thing and if the experiment did not work, it would not constitute a precedent. Nonetheless, the federal bureaucracy steadfastly refused to adapt its negotiating mandate to facilitate a locally developed solution to a serious problem. Once again, the ability of the federal government to stand in the way of progress by taking a 'leadership' role on a major public policy issue simply reinforces the value of managing the federation in accordance with the subsidiarity principle.

Federal government as facilitator and catalyst: understanding when and why federal involvement is appropriate

This argument for decentralization does not, however, mean that the federal government should have no role in the implementation of national policy: merely that it needs to recognize the limits of its abilities, if it is to contribute effectively to national policy making. The federal government has been effective in extending good policy ideas across the country. This is important, as citizens have a legitimate interest in ensuring that they have mobility throughout the country, so that they can take advantage of opportunities wherever they may exist, and some basic level of comparability of programs across the country supports this mobility. What the federal government is not skilled at, however, is actually designing and delivering programs that require significant physical infrastructure in many locales throughout the country and face-to-face interaction between service providers and individuals in need of a service. These tend to be the sorts of programs that require flexibility in design and delivery to adapt to local circumstances, local infrastructure and local knowledge that the federal government lacks.

Thus, the appropriate federal role in national policy should be to follow provincial and territorial leadership in their areas of jurisdiction, by facilitating policy innovations being experimented with in the provinces and territories, and acting as the catalyst to assist in the adoption by other provinces and territories of innovations that have been shown to be effective. This, of course, means that the federal government needs to commit itself to acting through intergovernmental mechanisms to ensure provincial and territorial concurrence before it acts in areas of provincial jurisdiction, rather than acting unilaterally. If the federal government were to function in this manner, it could add significant value to the policy process nationally, by supporting policy innovation and the spread and adaptation of good policy ideas without interfering in policy design and implementation.

Two examples of occasions when the federal government has played this role effectively should help to illustrate the point. The first is the classic Canadian social policy success story, that of the adoption of Medicare. Public hospital and medical insurance was originally experimented with in Saskatchewan, with hospital insurance being adopted in the province in 1947 and medical insurance being adopted in 1962. In both cases, only after an insurance system was implemented in Saskatchewan and some other provinces, did the federal government become involved in facilitating the adoption of comparable programs nationally, through the use of its spending power.

While federal fiscal support is critical to the financing of public health insurance in Canada, and the federal government uses its spending power to ensure some degree of comparability in the availability of hospital and physician services across the country, the federal government is not involved in providing, or even regulating, the actual delivery of hospital and health services in the provinces and territories. The reality in Canada is that we do not have a single public health care system, but thirteen health care systems, administered by provinces and territories, that are largely, but not entirely, comparable in their provision of hospital and physician services from public funds.

The federal government played a similar facilitative role in the development of the National Child Benefit in the 1990s, as part of the Social Policy Renewal process. In that case, the federal government decided to use the tax system to deliver a new Canada Child Tax Benefit (Warriner and Peach 2007: 78–79). Because this federal transfer would lead to an increase in the income of poor families, it would generate a savings for the provinces and territories in their social welfare costs. Through intergovernmental negotiation, it was agreed that the provinces and territories would reinvest these savings in other programs to assist in reducing child poverty (Ibid., 79). What particular programs the provinces and territories chose to invest the savings in was up to them, as no conditional federal transfers to the provinces and territories were involved in the scheme, but the provinces and territories committed to reporting to the Ministerial Council on Social Policy Renewal on the programs in which they reinvested their savings (Ibid., 91).

As with Medicare, this process did not result in a single national child benefit scheme identical across the country, but a scheme with a nationally administered core, the Canada Child Tax Benefit, and a variety of provincial and territorial initiatives designed to address the implications of child poverty in their jurisdictions in ways that were considered the most effective for those jurisdictions. While there remains a principled objection to the federal government establishing the Canada Child Tax Benefit in an area of provincial jurisdiction without prior consultation with provinces and territories, let alone provincial/territorial concurrence (Facal 2005: 2), the National Child Benefit arrangements at least did not put the federal government in the position of dictating, or even influencing, program design in the provinces and territories; what influence existed was created by an intergovernmental agreement on the reinvestment principle.

If government is about serving citizens, let's focus on objectives

There are several useful lessons in the experience of developing the National Child Benefit. Certainly, it demonstrates that intergovernmental mechanisms can sometimes be effective instruments of national policy. Another lesson of the National Child Benefit experience is that one way for the federal government to help manage intergovernmental coordination more effectively without returning to unilateral program definition is to focus not on defining and enforcing program details, but to focus instead on the objectives that governments are seeking to achieve for citizens.

It has become conventional wisdom in the performance management and public management literature that citizens are focused on results, and expect their governments to focus on achieving outcomes of importance to society as well. Bardach has described the central message of the "new public management" literature as the need to manage for results (Bardach 1998: 5). Similarly, Perri 6 et al. have commented that, "The first job of government is not to administer transactions, but to solve problems." (6 et al. 1999: 15). If the public management literature recommends a focus on results and program objectives for individual governments acting on their own in their areas of jurisdiction, logic dictates that governments acting in concert through intergovernmental mechanisms should also focus on objectives.

At the time of the negotiation of the Meech Lake Accord in 1987, the idea that the federal government would finance the activities of a province that did not participate in a national program but instead implemented a program that was 'compatible with the national objectives' was a matter of some controversy. Certainly the term 'compatible' is rather imprecise. That the focus of national policy making, especially in areas of provincial jurisdiction, should be on achieving a set of shared national objectives through whatever means prove most effective, taking due account of local circumstances and local knowledge, must, however, have progressed from being seen as a radically decentralist notion to a mainstream notion in the intervening twenty years, especially considering how public management theory has changed in that same period.

This is not a recipe for complete decentralization as much as a recipe for the more effective use of the mechanisms of intergovernmental relations in Canada to make truly national, rather than merely federal, policy. The national objectives would be the result of intergovernmental consultation and negotiation, but they must actually serve to set the direction of policy in the provinces and territories. Enforcement of these national objectives could be through a combination of the use of the federal spending power and intergovernmental mechanisms, which would be more in keeping with the federal government's existing conditional transfer arrangements and the terms of the Saskatoon Consensus position on SUFA, or it could be strictly through reporting and intergovernmental review, as with the National Child Benefit arrangement. The federal role in this model would be, at most, a fall-back in the face of the non-compliance of a province or territory in abiding by its intergovernmental commitments, tempered by an intergovernmental triggering mechanism, to make it a collective, rather than a unilateral, action, as Kennett has observed (Kennett 1998: 50). Such a role could also provide provinces and territories with the incentives to cooperate, rather than trigger a return to the "bad old days" of federal enforcement (Ibid., 51–52).

The focus on accomplishing a set of tangible objectives that would translate into improved outcomes for citizens on things that matter to them is the least that citizens have a right to expect from their governments. It should also serve the goal of fostering the mobility of citizens, whether by including a commitment to a mobility principle as one of the objectives of the program, or simply by securing a degree of comparability in programs across the country through the other objectives. In either case, program design could vary from province or territory to province or territory.

Improving intergovernmental coordination in federal jurisdictions: aboriginal policy and international agreements

Beyond restricting federal intervention in areas of provincial jurisdiction, Canada's policy environment would also be more coherent if the federal government were to use intergovernmental mechanisms before making policy in certain of its own areas of jurisdiction. Two key areas of federal jurisdiction in which greater intergovernmental cooperation is especially necessary are Aboriginal policy and the negotiation of international agreements. Both of these areas have been perennial sources of intergovernmental tension in Canada.

Despite the fact that the federal government has constitutional jurisdiction for "Indians and lands reserved for the Indians" under Section 91 (24) of the *Constitution Act, 1867*, the federal government continually resists providing programs, services and benefits to 'Indians' who do not live on reserves or Metis people, even in circumstances in which provinces and territories are prepared to work in partnership.

The only two standing programs that the federal government provides to First Nations people off reserves are some health benefits that are not publicly provided by provincial health care systems and support for post-secondary education. While the federal government does periodically establish programs that are accessible to all Aboriginal people, these tend to be small and have been more than offset by unilateral federal withdrawals of support, such as for social welfare for off-reserve First Nations people, that leave provinces and territories managing significant fiscal pressures. Given the extent to which the federal government has intervened in social policy fields that are clearly within provincial jurisdiction, continuing federal resistance to exercising its jurisdiction over Aboriginal people to its full extent is, to be polite, a curious situation, one that simply strengthens arguments for decentralization, or at least some enforceable federal commitment to intergovernmental coordination in exercising its constitutional jurisdiction.

A similar situation arises when the federal government exercises its authority to negotiate intergovernmental agreements without adequate prior consultation with, and involvement in the negotiations by provinces and territories. Under the Canadian constitutional structure, the federal government has the authority to represent Canada internationally, including in the negotiation of intergovernmental agreements, but it lacks the jurisdiction to implement those agreements to the extent that they implicate areas of provincial jurisdiction as a result of the Judicial Committee of the Privy Council's decision on Canada v. Attorney General of Ontario (the Labour Conventions case) 1937.

This, then, seems a circumstance ideally suited for meaningful intergovernmental consultation and coordination. Yet the federal government tends to treat intergovernmental consultation prior to engaging in negotiations on international agreements as little more than a formality, and provincial/territorial participation in delegations negotiating international agreements as something in federal discretion.

Needless to say, this severely undermines the ability of the federal government to secure provincial and territorial cooperation in implementing international agreements, though an intergovernmental agreement to implement any international agreements Canada signs would be an obvious *quid pro quo* for more thorough provincial and territorial involvement in the negotiation process. That this impasse has been a regular subject of intergovernmental tensions for decades and that provinces and territories must continue to raise it regularly (Council of the Federation 2008) is, to be frank, baffling.

Using what you have: replacing federal unilateralism with effective use of the mechanisms of intergovernmental relations

I have spoken repeatedly of the need to replace unilateral federal action with intergovernmental coordination. This is not a naive appeal, however; I certainly recognize that policy making through intergovernmental agreement has its challenges. As Kennett has noted, "the development and enforcement of national principles or standards through interprovincial or federal-provincial mechanisms represents a significant collective action problem, particularly if the threat of unilateral federal action is withdrawn." (Kennett 1998: 4) He goes on to identify three general obstacles to collective action, all of which affect intergovernmental policy making in Canada: incentives to free ride; incentives to cheat; and transaction costs accompanying coordination (Ibid., 20). Facal also commented that:

> Innovative social policy in modern, complex societies which recognize universal entitlements is extremely costly and all provinces except Alberta are cash-strapped. Their interests are so diverse they can hardly find significant common ground. Facing them is a federal juggernaut with huge financial clout, a clear view of what it wants to accomplish, and strong public support everywhere except Quebec (Facal 2005: 17).

Still, it is not as though Canada is bereft of experience in intergovernmental policy making or the mechanisms to manage intergovernmental coordination. A colleague in a provincial government has recently made the effort to determine exactly how many intergovernmental meetings take place in Canada in a year; the result was the discovery that there were over 800 multilateral meetings, across government departments and at all levels, in the year 2006–07. Governments have standing committees of ministers in virtually all areas of government and the experience of the Ministerial Council on Social Policy Renewal demonstrates that governments can establish effective committee structures when they conclude that they need to advance a significant reform agenda.

The problem, rather, is that we have not used what we have at our disposal as effectively as we could or should or structured those mechanisms in a way that maximizes

their utility. Some of the existing mechanisms of intergovernmental coordination, such as the Social Union Framework Agreement and the Council of the Federation, could
become valuable tools to improve intergovernmental policy making and constrain federal unilateralism or, indeed,
make it unnecessary. Given the Harper government's commitment to "open federalism" and its commitments to
constrain the use of the federal spending power (Canada
2008), the current climate seems to be a golden opportunity to engage in discussion of the reform of these two
mechanisms, in particular.

Facal has commented that "In no way, shape or form can
one conclude that SUFA has stimulated fruitful federal-provincial collaboration in social policy nor is it indicative of
a new era of cooperative federalism on any other count."
(Facal 2005: 16). Yet Facal himself once must have thought
that the Social Union Framework Agreement could work;
he was, after all, the Quebec Minister of Canadian Intergovernmental Relations at the time of its negotiation. If Canadian governments were to renegotiate SUFA, to return to
an approach consistent with the Saskatoon Consensus, it
could serve to generate a genuine constraint on the exercise
of the federal spending power and simultaneously secure
the commitments to mobility, accountability, and citizen
engagement in policy making that have been lost with the
dismissal of SUFA by all governments.

The Council of the Federation, which was established
by the Premiers in 2003, (Council of the Federation 2003),
could also be made more effective as an intergovernmental
policy-making body with a few critical reforms. One of the
most important reforms would be to invite the Prime Minister to participate and create, in effect, a provincial/ter-
ritorial council and a federal/provincial/territorial council,
as was done with the Ministerial Council on Social Policy
Renewal. Provinces and territories have long sought federal agreement to establish annual First Ministers conferences as a way to improve intergovernmental coordination;
having established the Council of the Federation, inviting
the Prime Minister to participate as well would seem to

be an ideal way to achieve this goal. The council should also make it a priority to reach out and communicate with Canadians about national policy issues, to end the federal government's monopoly in speaking for Canada. It could use this consultation to define a new approach to intergovernmental policy making and the legitimate roles and responsibilities of the federal and provincial/territorial orders of government; this could include establishing the utility and credibility of a revised SUFA.

To be an effective vehicle for managing a decentralization agenda and replacing federal unilateralism, the Council of the Federation also needs to revise its procedures in two critical ways. While the council should seek to achieve as broad a consensus as possible among the participating governments on the matters on its agenda, a rule that there must be consensus within the council before governments act within their own areas of jurisdiction would simply prevent the policy innovation that is one of the values of federalism. Indeed, one could go so far as to establish the rule that the federal government can support such innovation and its extension to other provinces and territories through the use of its spending power if, for example, the First Ministers of two-thirds of the provinces and territories with at least fifty percent of the population, acting in the federal/provincial/territorial Council of the Federation, concur. With a provision to allow opting out of a national program with compensation, this "minimum viable coalition" approach, as Kennett calls it, could allow for relatively rapid progress, in cooperation with the federal government if necessary, by those who seek it and the development of the sorts of asymmetries required to secure Quebec's concurrence to national programs and objectives (Kennett 1998: 53).

As well, the Council of the Federation needs the capacity to resolve disputes about the interpretation of agreements it reaches and enforce its agreements if intergovernmental mechanisms are to replace federal enforcement of national policy through the use of conditional grants. Kennett has noted, however, that it may be more fruitful and realistic to consider how intergovernmental institutions can alter the incentives that determine how provincial and territorial governments treat their intergovernmental obligations, rather than seeking hard enforcement mechanisms to make intergovernmental agreements binding (Ibid., 44). With reforms along these lines, the Council of the Federation could become the centrepiece of a new, intergovernmental approach to national policy making that would better respect our constitutional division of powers.

Canadian governments have at their disposal a wide variety of intergovernmental relation mechanisms to support a decentralized, yet coordinated, approach to national policy making. Some can be effective in their present form; some, such as the Ministerial Council on Social Policy Renewal, have fallen into disuse; and others, such as SUFA and the Council of the Federation, need reform to become more effective policy making vehicles. They have this potential, however, if they are treated seriously by all governments as the decision-making tools that can replace the unilateral exercise of the federal spending power as the driver of national policies.

Conclusion

The federal government has played, and can continue to play, a useful role in the development of national policies, but it needs to understand the limits of its role and abilities. The federal government is at its best when it facilitates policy innovation at the provincial and territorial levels, and helps to extend innovations that have been proven effective to other provinces and territories; but it is at its worst when it seeks to lead policy development by unilaterally dictating the details of policies designed in Ottawa, requiring them to be implemented across the country, and enforcing their terms through conditional grants. Such behaviour both undermines our constitutional structure and makes for ineffective policy because it fails to recognize the valuable role that local knowledge plays in policy design and implementation.

Rather than either relying on federal unilateralism to make national policy or abandoning national policy entirely, Canadian governments can make policy through intergovernmental consultation and coordination. They already have at their disposal a wide variety of mechanisms to assist them in that task. While intergovernmental policy making is not without its challenges, as is any collective action exercise, Canadian governments have demonstrated in the past that they can undertake meaningful policy reforms through intergovernmental mechanisms.

Thus, decentralization need not mean balkanization of the country and the end of national policy, as some have suggested. My view has never been that radical decentralization is needed in Canada. There is a purpose in having a country and the opportunities that being part of Canada has brought to its citizens have, in many ways, made the country the envy of many nations. Yet, equally important is the fact that Canada is a federal country; we need to respect the reasons we are a federal country when we act at the national level, if we are to retain the loyalty of all citizens. Too often, the federal fact of Canada has been more 'honoured in the breach than in the observance' by past federal governments. As a committed federalist who has directly experienced the perverse effects of such federal behaviour, I am left preferring the 'evil' of decentralization, while hoping that effective intergovernmental coordination will allow us to realize the benefits of national policy without abandoning our commitment to the federal division of powers.

Endnotes

[1] The comments and conclusions in this chapter, however, are strictly my own and reflect my personal views and experiences as an official with, at various times, the Government of Ontario, the Government of the Yukon, and the Government of Saskatchewan, as well as a scholar of federalism and intergovernmental relations in Canada; in no way should they be construed as representing the position of the Government of Canada or any other government.

References

6, Perri et al. 1999. *Governing in the Round: Strategies for Holistic Government*. London: Demos.

Ajzenstat, Janet et al. 2003. *Canada's Founding Debates*. Toronto: University of Toronto Press.

Bardach, Eugene 1998. *Getting Agencies to Work Together: the Practice and Theory of Managerial Craftsmanship*. Consensus Report on the Constitution 1992, August 28.

Canada 1937. Supreme Court of Canada. Canada v Attorney General of Ontario (the Labour Conventions case) A.C. 326.

_____ 1987. *Constitutional Accord* (Meech Lake Accord). Ottawa.

_____ 1998 (August 6). "Framework Agreement on Canada's Social Union." News release. Saskatoon, Saskatchewan: 39th Annual Premier's Conference. Available at www.scics.gc.ca/cinfo98/85007010_e.html [consulted April 20, 2008].

_____ 2008 (November 19). "Protecting Canada's Future." Speech from the Throne. Available at www.sft-ddt.gc.ca/eng/media.asp?id=1364 [consulted April 20, 2009].

Consensus Report on the Constitution 1992 (August 28). Charlottetown: Final Report. Available at www.solon.org/Constitutions/Canada/English/Proposals/CharlottetownConsensus. html) [consulted March 26, 2010].

Council of the Federation 2003 (December 5). *Council of the Federation Founding Agreement*. Available at www.councilofthefederation.ca/pdfs/COF_agreement.pdf [consulted April 20, 2009].

Council of the Federation 2008 (July 18). "Trade: Building on our Strengths in Canada and Abroad." News release. Quebec City, QC. Available at www.councilofthefederation.ca/pdfs/COMMUNIQUE_TRADE_clean.pdf [consulted April 20, 2009].

Facal, Joseph 2005. *Social Policy and Intergovernmental Relations in Canada: Understanding the Failure of SUFA from a Quebec Perspective*. SIPP Public Policy Paper 32. Regina: Saskatchewan Institute of Public Policy.

Hueglin, Thomas O. 2007. "The Principle of Subsidiarity: Tradition–Practice—Relevance." In *Constructing Tomorrow's Federalism: New Perspectives on Canadian Governance*, ed. Ian Peach. Winnipeg: University of Manitoba Press, 210–213.

Kennett, Steven 1998. *Securing the Social Union: A Commentary on the Decentralized Approach*. Kingston, ON: Institute of Intergovernmental Relations.

Madison, James 1788 (February 6). "The Federalist No. 51: The Structure of the Government Must Furnish the Proper Checks and Balances Between the Different Departments." *Independent Journal*.

Robson, William and Daniel Schwanen 1999. *The Social Union: Too Flawed to Last*. Toronto: C.D. Howe Institute.

Smiley, Donald 1983. "A Dangerous Deed: The Constitution Act, 1982." In *And No One Cheered: Federalism, Democracy and the Constitution Act*, eds. Keith Banting and Richard Simeon. Toronto: Methuen, 74–95.

Warriner, William E. and Ian Peach 2007. *Canadian Social Policy Renewal, 1994-2000*. Halifax: Fernwood Publishing.

Chapter 3

The Theoretical Defence of Decentralization

Gérard Bélanger

Introduction

By its very nature, a federal system of government embodies a contradiction. In a federal state (such as Canada, the United States or Germany), authority is constitutionally divided, with legal jurisdiction being given to the national government over some matters, to sub-national governments for others, while some are shared. As a result, a federal system amounts to a kind of decentralized centralization.

For some, 'decentralization' and 'centralization' can be thought of as the two ends of a continuum. For me, the terms truly represent a dichotomy: two very divergent dynamics with a very unstable middle.

This chapter proceeds in several stages. First, the decentralization-centralization dichotomy and their divergent dynamics are presented. Second, the same problem is shown to apply in the study of federal systems: two opposing concepts of federalism ensue. Third, the uses of the two (opposing) formulations suggest a number of propositions. The conclusion suggests that Canada is operating in the unstable middle and that a bet on decentralization is the better alternative.

Decentralized and centralized economic systems

Economic systems are often thought of as occupying a place on a continuum between pure decentralization and pure centralization. While, in principle, the whole range of possibilities along the continuum might be regarded as possible, the dynamics of the polar cases are such that sustainable workable options are likely to be located only close to the polar positions. There is no way to decentralize centralization by fifty percent without inconsistencies and instability.

Decentralization and centralization

Decentralization allows for freedom of choice, flexibility, diverse actions, autonomy and the accountability of decision makers. It relies very largely on market institutions to allocate resources. It underpins the operations not only of private companies, but also of non-profit organizations, of producers' and consumers' cooperatives and even of households and families.

To be effective in normal circumstances, decentralized arrangements require an appropriate legal basis, such as well-defined property rights. But such arrangements can generate inefficiencies and/or unacceptable outcomes as a result of the existence of external and large-scale economies, asymmetric information, public goods, monopolistic powers or an income distribution that is seen as unsatisfactory. As a result, despite the advantages of decentralization, economists have developed a whole arsenal of arguments to justify central and governmental interventions.

Unfortunately the countless ways in which decentralization may generate inefficiencies or failures have encouraged some economists to try to justify government intervention in virtually every activity. This is not unlike the case of the Roman emperor who, in judging a singing competition between two individuals, listened to the first, and then quickly awarded the prize to the second without bothering to listen to him, on the presumption that he could not be worse.

Justifying governmental intervention on the basis of market inefficiencies alone focuses only on the waste and inefficiency of decentralized decision making. It ignores the corresponding inefficiencies and waste generated by centralized interventions, such as little user accountability, standardization and 'cartelization' of services, or the relative suppression of experimentation and flexibility, to mention just a few. The presumption is that the mechanisms for resource allocation in a centralized system (i.e., political processes, elections, lobbying, etc.) are more capable than the market to allocate resources so as to satisfy citizens' preferences. The promoters of centralized mechanisms conveniently presume that the centralized authority is a benevolent and omniscient despot whose sole goal is the well-being of citizens. As a result, deficiencies in the political processes are deemed to be unimportant, and the mechanisms creating this 'magnanimous' authority are not seen as warranting examination.

Glimpses at the Canadian case
The expanded role of the public sector in the 20th century, coupled with an acceleration of economic growth, has had important impacts on Canada. Direct public expenditures grew from 15.0 percent and 21.3 percent of gross domestic product (GDP), between 1926 and 1950, to approximately 50.0 percent between 1985 and 1995. In 2007, it was 39.0 percent. But these numbers do not give a complete measure of the government impact. For example, the substitution of a child tax credit for family allowances in the 1990s transformed a direct government expenditure into an indirect one (i.e., loss of public income), thereby reducing the direct expenditures to GDP ratio. But it did not connote any reduction in the relative importance of the state.

To get a clearer (but still incomplete) picture of the government sector, the tax expenditures (implicit in tax reductions) must be added in. As a case in point, in 1992, actual expenditures in Canada amounted to 45 percent of the economy. If one were to add the 'implicit expenditures', that percentage would increase by 50 percent, amounting to 67 percent. Moreover, there are countless modes of government intervention that modify relative prices: subsidies, taxes, customs duties, quotas, public enterprises, preferential procurement policies, traditional or social regulations and prohibitions.

Finally, government regulation is omnipresent in the world today. For example the federal government of the United States publishes a daily *Federal Register* that lists all the rules and regulations proposed or finalized. In 2007, this publication totalled 72,090 pages. However, as Allan Meltzer observes: "The first principle of regulation is: Lawyers and politicians write rules; and markets develop ways to circumvent these rules without violating them" (Meltzer 2007: 14). The indirect cost to the economy that this degree of regulation imposes is undoubtedly considerable (presuming that regulation is a legitimate government tool that can be effective and beneficial in some cases).

Is decentralization doomed to fail? Maybe not, but...

First, decentralization requires some 'rules of the game' to function, and most of these rules are produced by government—by some central authority. In other words, to foster more decentralization, some centralization is needed.

Second, decentralization faces criticisms about the frequent errors and scandals that beset the kind of experimentation that is required by today's world—a world that is full of pitfalls and requires constant compromise and navigation through uncertain or troubled waters. The incomplete privatization of the former Hydro-Ontario and the establishment of a wholesale market in electricity required almost a thousand pages of legal dispositions. With the current focus on blaming not learning, coping with these negative observations can be very difficult and costly. 'Armchair quarterbacks' abound.

Third, attempts by governments to withdraw from certain activities through privatization can be attacked as being "more about raising money than about promoting enterprise" as *The Economist* has observed is the case "[i]n most of 'Europe'" (*The Economist* 2002: 63). So a certain inertia factor sets in once government has invaded a realm of activities.

Finally, the benefits of decentralization have the characteristics of a public good: common consumption and problems without excluding anyone lead to 'free riders'. For
example, faced without competition, companies deliver
goods and services more efficiently. Notwithstanding this,
however, each company has an incentive to lobby for government protection to increase its profits (the 'ideal' being to
be protected in a world where others are in competition).

Milton Friedman referred to this as *The Business Community's Suicidal Impulse:*

> I do blame businessmen when, in their political activi-
> ties, individual businessmen and their organizations take
> positions that are not in their own self-interest and that
> have the effect of undermining support for free private
> enterprise. In that respect, businessmen tend to be schizo-
> phrenic. When it comes to their own businesses, they
> look a long time ahead, thinking of what the business is
> going to be like 5 to 10 years from now. But when they get
> into the public sphere and start going into the problems
> of politics, they tend to be very short-sighted (Friedman
> 1999: 6).

Nonetheless, centralization is not immune from criticism.
The public sector imposes rules on private companies that it
circumvents itself in a number of areas (employee pensions,
financial statements and construction holidays).

Public–private partnerships as a decentralized centralization experiment

Decentralized centralization has been experimented with,
but the evidence is not very encouraging.

In fact, in the area of public-private partnerships (PPP),
there appear to be misgivings. The PPP substitutes a longer-
term contract for construction, maintenance, management
and financing of a project instead of a short-term request
for proposal to construct a building. A brief mention of their
difficulties can be found in the conclusion of an analysis of
ten Canadian PPPs:

> The ten case studies indicate that the potential benefits of
> P3s are often outweighed by high contracting costs due
> to opportunism generated by goal conflict. Those costs
> are particularly high when construction or operating
> complexity is high, revenue uncertainty (use-risk) is high,
> both of these risks have been transferred to the private-
> sector partner, and contract management effectiveness is
> poor. In infrastructure projects, it rarely makes sense to
> try to transfer large amounts of risk to the private sector
> (Vining and Boardman 2008: 9).

The bottom line is that each of decentralization and centralization has its own dynamics and each has effects that
can be negative, positive or both at the same time. But there
are grounds for pessimism in trying to marry the divergent
objectives of private sector and public sector partners: the
goals of maximizing profits at the same time as achieving
political objectives. Efforts to pursue this third way could
prove unrealistic.

The difficulty may be synthesized more colourfully. Dogs
bark and cats meow. Too many proposals trying to find a middle ground are not unlike trying to make a dog meow or a cat
bark. It seems that sooner or later however, the true nature of
the animal re-emerges despite much training effort. In effect,
there is a 'no man's land' between the two polar positions.

Abstract federalism or a concrete reality

The decentralization-centralization debate about Canadian
federalism generates the same type of problems.

Two frameworks
Two different approaches (frames of reference) to the decentralization-centralization debate in the world of federalism
are in good currency.

The first approach ('the conventional approach') focuses
on the formal division of labour between different levels of
government. It is an abstract and somewhat romanticized

conceptualization of benevolent political despots—with the sole goal of citizens' well-being—fighting market inefficiencies and unacceptable societal outcomes.

The economist Wallace Oates uses this framework when describing federalism:

> From an economic standpoint, the obvious attraction of the federal form of government is that it combines the strengths of unitary government with those of decentralization. Each level of government, rather than attempting to perform all the functions of the public sector, does what it can do best. The central government, presumably accepts primary responsibility for stabilizing the economy, for achieving the most equitable distribution of income, and for providing certain public goods that influence significantly the welfare of all members of society. Complementing these operations, subcentral governments can supply those public goods and services that are of primary interest only to the residents of their respective jurisdiction. In this way, a federal form of government offers the best promise of a successful resolution of the problems that constitute the economic raison d'être of the public sector. It is in this sense that federalism may, in economic terms, be describes as the optimal form of government (Oates 1972: 14–15).

He picked up de Tocqueville's 1835 idea: "It is to unite the diverse advantages resulting from the greatness and the smallness of nations that the federal system was created" (de Tocqueville 2000: 152).

The second approach ('the public choice approach') involves a concrete analysis of the actual experiences of federalism in terms of the 'rules of the game', with assumptions about the importance of incentive-reward systems, and vertical competition between levels of government.

The political scientist Riker leans in the direction of greater realism when he talks about American federalism: "In function after function there is in fact no division of authority between constituent governments and the centre, but rather a mingling" (Riker 1975: 104). He adds this metaphor:

The American form of government is often, but errone-
ously, symbolized by a three-layer cake. A far more accurate image is the rainbow or marble cake, characterized
by an inseparable mingling of different coloured ingredi-
ents, the colors appearing in vertical and diagonal strands
and unexpected whirls. As colors are mixed in the marble
cake, so functions are mixed in the federal system (Ibid.).

Using the 'conventional' framework

There are significant drawbacks to using the 'conventional'
framework to reflect on the decentralization-centralization
debate about Canadian federalism.

For example, using this framework, Canada would seem
to be already highly decentralized in many ways. Data on
developed countries (those of federal systems, in particular)
reveal a relatively significant decentralization of the Canadian
public sector. By a large margin, Canada is in the forefront in
terms of the share of revenues and expenses of non-central
governments in the overall public sector (figure 3.1).

**Figure 3.1   Sub-national shares of revenue and expenditure
in percent of total government, 2003/04**

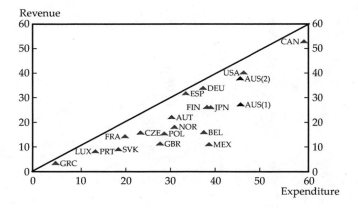

Note: The two data points for Australia show 1) the goods and services tax
(GST) considered as a grant, and 2) GST considered as a state tax.

Source: OECD, *OECD Economic Surveys. Australia* 2006, Paris: OECD,
2006, p. 75.

Figure 3.2   Shares of provincial and local government revenues in total public sector revenues in federal countries, 2004 (%)

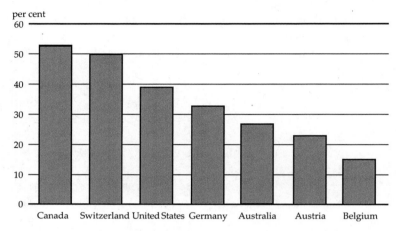

Source: Department of Finance Canada, *Budget 2006. Restoring Fiscal Balance in Canada,* Ottawa, 2006, p. 94.

Figure 3.3   Share of autonomous revenues in provincial and local revenues in federal countries, 2004 (%)

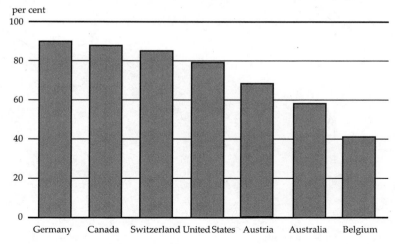

Source: Department of Finance Canada, *Budget 2006. Restoring Fiscal Balance in Canada,* Ottawa, 2006, p. 95.

If we limit ourselves to the seven federal systems, Canada is first in terms of the share of total revenues of provincial and local governments relative to the overall public sector receipts (figure 3.2) and in second place for the share of autonomous revenue in regional and local revenue (figure 3.3).

This way of looking at things is somewhat surreal

The national/sub-national partitioning of public sector expenditures and revenues is a useful but incomplete indicator of the evolution of centralization in a federation. For instance, the significant decrease of the federal dollar contribution to financing provincial health expenditures, from the end of the 1980s to the end of the 1990s, in no way reduced the restrictive nature of the *Canada Health Act*.

No wonder some key stakeholders find the results of this sort of analysis deeply (and unacceptably) unsatisfactory.

In Quebec in 2005, governmental transfers represented 10.2 percent of total revenues for the municipal sector. Does this mean that we ought to conclude that there is a great deal of autonomy at this level of government? The answer is not so clear—it is complicated by the presence of a significant regulatory framework imposed by the government of Quebec on various activities of the municipalities.

Moreover, the formal system does not fully define government behaviour. The Constitution does not constrain levels of government to a precise division of labour. In Canada, with the growth of public expenditures post World War II, extremely broad powers were granted to the central government. According to a document of the Federal-Provincial Relations Office of the federal government, there has been "a widespread, if not general, breakdown of traditional constitutional fences" (Canada 1979: 9–10). This same document also said:

> Although the frequency of the procedures and practices that we describe varied, they were sufficiently widespread to warrant the following observations:

a) initial departmental responses to the question about the constitutional basis for the activity under review indicated that the majority of federal public servants concerned did not know what the relevant authority was;

b) further enquiries at subsequent meetings, suggested that in many cases, if not the majority, the question of the distribution of powers had not been thoroughly considered when the activities were undertaken;

c) more often than not, departments eventually indicated that the constitutional authority for activities was one of more of the following: the Peace, Order and Good Government (POGG) clause of section 91, even though in certain cases there was no enabling legislation justifying the reference to POGG; the federal spending power, derived in part from sections 91.1A and 91.3; or, least frequently, Parliament's power to declare works to be for the general advantage of Canada, section 92.10.(c);

d) the British North America Act, and particularly the sections setting out the distribution of powers, did not appear to be a part either of the formal training of the public servants concerned, or, more significantly, of their governmental experience (Ibid.).

Is the central government a benevolent or a malevolent authority?

A focus on formal federal systems like Canada's that would presume that the central government is serving the national interest well is deeply flawed. It assumes, in effect, that, except for lack of information on the intensity of preferences for strictly local services, a unitary system of government would be the optimal choice (since there would be no other reason for a politically divided government structure).

Geoffrey Brennan and James Buchanan express the counterargument very well:

There would seem to be no reason why strictly localized public goods should not be provided by supralocal governmental units, which might, of course, decentralize administratively as the relevant externality limits dictate. In other words, the conventional theory offers no basis for deriving an upper bound on the size of political jurisdictions. There is no analysis that demonstrates the superiority of a genuinely federal political structure over a unitary structure, with the latter administratively decentralized.

This result is not, in itself surprising when we recognize that the 'economic theory' of federalism is no different from standard normative economics in its implicit assumptions about politics. The normative advice proffered by the theory is presumably directed toward the benevolent despotism that will implement the efficiency criteria. No support can be generated for a politically divided governmental structure until the prospects for nonidealized despotism are acknowledged. Once government comes to be modeled either as a complex interaction process akin to that analyzed in standard public choice or, as in this book, in terms of leviathan-like behaviour, an argument for a genuinely federal structure can be developed. Further, the normative theory that emerges can be as 'economic' as the conventional one. The individual, at the initial stage of constitutional deliberation, may find it 'efficient' to decentralize and to disperse the effective taxing power as between the central and the subordinate units of government (Brennan and Buchanan 1980: 174–5).

Using the public choice framework

In reality then, federalism reflects the same problems mentioned in the earlier discussion regarding the centralization-decentralization dichotomy: problems that the 'conventional' framework ignores. Two examples, one relating to the national common market and the other Quebec's wasteful level of public expenditures, illustrate these difficulties clearly.

1) *The federal source of balkanization*

For two hundred years, economists have preached the virtues of free trade as a source of well-being (see for example, the two important books published in 1776 by Abbot Étienne Bonnot de Condillac and Adam Smith). Free trade allows for a more extended market, as well as a reduction in costs, thanks to a better division of labour and an enhanced competitive environment. This is especially significant for a small region. Indeed, it is particularly in the interest of small regions to specialize since, even in the short term, it has no monopolistic power in the international market. In addition, protectionism practised by other jurisdictions does not justify recourse to protectionist measures, because free trade, even unilaterally, raises the total income of the region.

All federal constitutions prevent regional governments from establishing tariff barriers to products imported from other countries or regions of the same country. International and inter-regional commerce falls exclusively within the central government's jurisdiction, which can only impose tariff barriers on imported products. In this way, federal constitutions aim to create a common market within their territory, i.e., free trade in goods and services.

Nonetheless, tariff barriers are only some of the obstacles to trade and are a form whose relative importance is waning due to various negotiations, principally within the context of GATT (General Agreement on Tariffs and Trade) and now the WTO (World Trade Organization). Today, protectionism takes the form instead of non-tariff barriers, especially quotas for different products, subsidies for indigenous producers, preferential procurement policies and, finally, regulation of various goods and services. Therefore, the multiplicity of such governmental interventions contributes to the dismantling of the common market within a federation. The consequence is that, for a number of decades, we have been witnessing the balkanization of the Canadian economy.

Balkanization is the outcome of governmental intervention dissociating the price of regional goods and services from the regional costs of production. A balkanizing effect is also present when the prices of goods and services offered by the public sector are distorted. In modifying relative regional prices, public intervention both confers variable benefits and imposes variable costs on people in the regions, thereby fostering balkanization.

As an example of this, consider the federal government's grant of a number of billions of dollars to the nuclear industry—something that benefited Ontario considerably. In fact it has all but two of the nuclear reactors in operation in Canada. As a result, this assistance can only be seen as a source of balkanization of the Canadian economy; it distorted the relative or regional prices in the territory. Consequently, Quebec's advantage over Ontario in terms of electricity was artificially diminished.

Balkanization of the Canadian economy is not only a consequence of provincial protectionist policies: it is also the result of many central government programs that distort relative regional prices. It is not ridiculous to advance the hypothesis that the central government has a more significant balkanizing effect than other orders of government because its discretionary power is greater than theirs, since it is less subject to competition.

For example, the editors of a work on balkanization in Canada wrote:

> In fact, it is difficult to predict that central or unitary governments will be less prone to distort internal trade flows than lower levels of government. The evidence presented in this book suggests the opposite (Trebilcock et al. 1983: 158).

Thus while both federal and provincial policies distort internal trade flows, the former has more discretionary power than the latter and as a result has more impact.

2) Federal largesse as the source for Quebec wasting of taxpayers' money

Consider as well, the case of Quebec's paradoxical public expenditures. Despite the fact that Quebec is considered a

poor province, the government of Quebec offers its population more generous services than other provinces, such
as the daycare program at seven dollars a day and modest
tuition fees for post-secondary education.

This phenomenon is generally explained by Quebecers'
preferences that seem more European-inspired than North
American. I see it instead as a result of the sizeable and
unjustifiable equalization payments that the federal government transfers to Quebec.

In 2008–2009, the government of Quebec received eight
billion dollars in equalization payments, an amount equal
to 16 percent of its own revenue. The Ontario government
did not receive a cent. Is this difference justified? At first
sight, the response is 'yes'. According to the two criteria of
GDP and personal income per capita, in 2006, there was a
gap of between 12 and 16 percent in favour of Ontario. Quebec was, therefore, relatively poor.

These data, however, do not consider the differential cost
of living between the two provinces. According to comparative indices of retail prices for October 2006, the cost of living in Montreal was 14.7 percent less than in Toronto. This
means that the real gap in average income between the two
provinces is negligible. This equality in real income should
not be surprising despite a generally more rapid expansion
in Ontario than in Quebec and in Toronto than in Montreal.
The Quebec economy corresponds to the economic model of
a 'small economy', where an adjustment takes place gradually by a relative movement of the population and through
a convergence of real incomes.

What has the relative population movement in the recent
past been? From 1951 to 2006, Quebec's share of the Canadian population went from 28.9 to 23.5 percent while that
of Ontario rose from 32.8 to 38.9 percent. Quebec's share of
population decreased on average by one tenth of one percent per year.

Given the real income of Quebec and Ontario, the differential of eight billion dollars in equalization payments
between the two provinces is not justifiable at all. One
question remains: why isn't this major 'gift' from the fed-

eral government transferred to taxpayers via a reduced tax burden? A number of empirical studies have concluded that unconditional subsidies to lower level administrations, such as equalization payments to provinces, lead to equivalent increases in expenditures. This has been termed the 'flypaper effect' (whereby money sticks wherever it lands). In addition, equalization payments lessen the burden provinces shoulder for inefficient policies, such as the dissipation of rents from natural resources. In fact, they encourage provinces to impose higher rates of taxation. For instance, with the new equalization formula, the government of Quebec has every incentive to minimize payments received from Hydro-Québec (dividends and hydraulic royalties). Each dollar of these payments reduces its equalization benefits by thirty-eight cents. In recent years, strangely, it has done the opposite.

A more general argument along these lines has been made by some economists:

> Generally speaking, scholars have not found federalism to lower budgets and restrain public spending, and its precise competitive inducements are still a matter of conjecture…. Furthermore, federalism has its costs. Grants from higher levels of government encourage lower governments to increase spending, so by fiscal 'laundering' it can defeat, to some extent, the exit constraint. Also, many tiers of governments mean more politicians who answer to special interest groups desiring more public expenditures…. Because of such costs of complication and incoherence, small homogeneous states will use it less, while large heterogeneous states may use it more (Borcherding and Lee 2006: 126; Breton 1996; Mueller 2003; Cullis and Jones 1998).

The 'bizarreries' of centralization

A reason for the growing centralized power within federations and of increased standardization of services across the territory are due to the fact that the central authority more easily raises taxes because it is less subject to competition.

Where it lacks the power to intervene unilaterally, it is able to buy power over other levels of government by bribing them. The same rationale explains the loss of local government's autonomy.

Evidence of growing centralization such as this does not mean that the federal government is doing its job well. Indeed it might even be the reverse. When an organization operates in two different markets (being the only provider in the first one and being subject to competition in the second), it will have the tendency to be more concerned with the latter. In the former, it has a captive market.

The same reasoning applies in the context of vertical competition within a federal system. In its search for votes to be re-elected, the federal government is in a position of monopoly in providing strictly national goods, such as national defence. The central government is the designated provider of goods that remain far from the immediate concerns of citizens. Nevertheless, it is still interested in getting closer to citizens through offering regional, local or even private goods because it is more profitable in electoral terms. The result is that the central government tends to neglect truly national questions. There is a greater incentive for the federal government to get involved in providing regional and local goods even where there are no national ramifications.

As a case in point, the federal government assumes responsibility for a significant share of improvements to the Québec–Saguenay highway, an investment in which it is hard to find a national interest.

Vertical competition, inherent to the federal system through the presence of different levels of administration, triggers a race for subsidies on the part of lower authorities. I live in a region (Quebec City) where this dynamic is well developed. During the federal elections of January 2006, two major media posed the following question to their readers/listeners: "Has Québec received its fair share from the federal government?" One might wonder about the conception of federalism underlying this mass appeal. For my part, I saw in this "the role of a distributor of gifts rivalling Santa Claus" (Bélanger 2006: A-16).

Subsidies from the higher level of government to lower authorities alter incentives. Since subsidies are directed to capital expenditures more than to current or operational expenditures, they bias decisions in favour of subsidized activities. For example, because the government of Quebec offers a subsidy of 50 percent (it has been as high as 75 percent in the past) for the purchase of new vehicles, without contributing to operational expenses, regional public transit authorities are encouraged to replace their fleet more rapidly, thus lessening the life expectancy of a bus. Indeed, they must assume all the costs associated with an aging fleet. This phenomenon fosters what can be called disposable or 'Kleenex' buses.

This same dynamic is at play when senior level governments finance municipal infrastructure renewal, such as sewage and waterworks systems. A bungalow's owner knows full well that the asphalt shingles on his roof will need to be replaced periodically, and that it is in his own interest to plan ahead for the necessary future expenditure. The same kind of logic does not seem to be the case for municipal corporations, who rely on catastrophes to obtain better subsidies from higher level governments.

All this suggests that to allow for the growth of decentralization in a federal system like Canada's, there is a need for a strong central government to resist unreasonable demands for subsidies from lower order governments (that always want autonomy over spending without having to take the responsibility of raising the revenue themselves). Politically, this is unlikely.

General considerations

These two approaches lead to three general propositions:

a) The two approaches are very different, indeed contradictory.

According to the 'conventional' approach, public interventions are exogenous to political processes: they stem from decisions of a sort of benevolent despot whose only concern is the common good. In contrast, in the 'public choice' framework, governmental decisions are the product of agents pursuing their own interests.

These different points of departure lead to different conclusions on the division of powers. The first approach shows a clear bias towards centralization since only the central despot can maximize the national interest, as opposed to the parochial spirit of regional authorities. Indeed, the conclusions follow logically from the enlightened despot assumption.

On the other hand, starting with individuals seeking their own interests, the public choice approach leans in favour of decentralization, in order to facilitate the expression of the population's varied preferences and also to prevent the 'cartelization' of the public sector.

b) The conventional approach generates specific conclusions based on weak grounds.

If centralization is essential in seeking the common good, one might wonder why there are so few efficient policies originating from the central government. Hasn't this approach come up morally empty-handed?

In response to the possible imperfections of decentralization, this approach suggests centralization, but without in turn examining the failures of this centralization. As some economists have said:

> If federalism can combine the advantages of small and great nations, so too can it combine their disadvantages. Fiscal federalism has made considerable progress from its beginnings in the analysis of very specific questions concerning fiscal policy, but it still has some way to go before it can claim to offer a fully rounded account of federalism from an economic perspective (Brennan and Hamlin 1998: 149).

To be of real interest, the conventional approach must examine critically the mechanisms or processes that give rise to the benevolent central authority to which it invokes as a *deus ex machina*.

c) The public choice approach defines the questions more realistically, but its conclusions remain vague.

It brings together research using traditional economic methodology (i.e., economic agents pursuing their own interests) to explain government actions. Government decisions are not exogenous and they need to be explained. The role of the 'social scientist' no longer consists in advising the benevolent despot (or the prince), but in explaining the impact of different decision-making rules. Consequently, the relevant question becomes the following: what mechanisms can improve policies and bring them nearer the real preferences of heterogeneous citizens?

The responses to such a general question are imprecise and will probably remain so for a long time. In fact, knowledge about salient points, such as the imperfections of the political market or the role of bureaucratic competition, remains rather undeveloped.

But, despite the enormous gaps in our knowledge, the public choice approach is more realistic and seems more helpful as an approximation of the functioning of real-life federalism. It has also a strong inclination towards the major incentive system of competition and therefore favours decentralization.

One might be somewhat reassured by the fact that even though the public choice framework is only cautiously supporting decentralization, this is in line with what has been the principal teaching of economics for more than two centuries.

Conclusion

Decentralized federalism is a way to ensure a more open political system. Such openness is highly desirable for the reasons mentioned above; however, it remains constantly under threat by centralizing forces.

Weingast has defined this political dilemma of the economic system as follows:

> A government strong enough to protect property rights
> and enforce contracts is also strong enough to confiscate
> the wealth of its citizens. Thriving markets require not only
> the appropriate system of property rights and a law of con-
> tracts, but a secure political foundation that limits the abil-
> ity of the state to confiscate wealth (Weingast 1995: 1).

The same sort of dilemma permeates every federal system. A true confederation requires much discretion at the
junior levels of government and credible limits to the intervention or hegemony of central government. But a central
government powerful enough to limit its own interventions
is obviously capable of intruding into all issue domains, and
self-imposed limits of a constitutional sort are hardly likely
to stop actions by the central government, dictated by the
exigencies of real-life federalism. The fundamental threat to
federalism is therefore not undue decentralization, but the
centralizing thrust of the political dynamics.

So if one were to draw from our analysis a cautious conclusion, it would be that it is best to err on the side of decentralization.

References

Bélanger, Gérard 2006 (January 18). "Québec a-t-elle sa juste part du fé-
    déral?" *Le Soleil*, 110: 20: A-16.
Borcherding, Thomas and Dong Lee 2006. "The Supply Side of
    Democratic Government: A Brief Survey." In *The Elgar Companion to
    Public Economics*, eds. F. Otl and R. J. Cinula. Chettenham, UK: Edward
    Elgar, 115–130.
Brennan, Geoffrey and James M. Buchanan 1980. *The Power to Tax:
    Analytical*
Foundations of a Fiscal Constitution. Cambridge, UK: Cambridge University
    Press.
Brennan, Geoffrey and Alan Hamlin 1998. "Fiscal Federalism." In *The
    New Palgrave Dictionary of Economics and the Law*, ed. P. Newman, vol. 2.
    London: Macmillan, 144–150.
Breton, Albert 1996. *Competitive Governments: An Economic Theory of Politics
    and Public Finance*. Cambridge UK: Cambridge University Press.

Canada 1979. *Interim Report on Relations Between the Government of Canada and the Province of Quebec, 1967-1977*. Ottawa: Privy Council, Federal-Provincial Relations Office, 9–10.

Cullis, John and Philip Jones 1998. *Public Finance and Public Choice*. New York: Oxford University Press.

de Tocqueville, A. 2000. *Democracy in America*. Chicago: University of Chicago Press.

Friedman, Milton 1999 (March–April). "The Business Community's Suicidal Impulse." *Cato Policy Report*, 21: 2: 6.

LeGrand, Julian 2007. *The Other Invisible Hand: Delivering Public Services through Choice and Competition*. Princeton, NJ: Princeton University Press.

Meltzer, Allan H. 2007 (March 27). "Regulatory Overkill." *The Wall Street Journal*, p. A-14.

Mueller, Dennis C. 2003. *Public Choice III*. Cambridge UK: Cambridge University Press.

Oates, Wallace E. 1972. *Fiscal Federalism*. New York: Harcourt Brace Jovanovich.

"Privatization in Europe: Coming Home to Roost." 2002 (June 27). *The Economist*, 63.

Riker, R. William 1975. "Federalism." In *Handbook of Political Science*, ed. F. I. Greenstein, vol. 5, "Government Institutions and Processes." Reading, MA: Addison-Wesley.

Trebilcock, Michael J. et al. 1983. *Federalism and the Canadian Economic Union*. Toronto: University of Toronto Press.

Vining, Aidan R. and Anthony E. Boardman 2008 (March). "Public-Private Partnership in Canada: Theory and Evidence." *Canadian Public Administration*, 51: 1: 9–44.

Weingast, Barry R. 1995 (April). "The Economic Role of Political Institution: Market-Preserving Federalism and Economic Development." *Journal of Law, Economics, and Organization*, 11: 1: 1.

Part II:
The Normative Case

Chapter 4

Beyond Centralization: How to Liberate Federalism?

Hugh D. Segal

Introduction

Bargains reached between accountable politicians often include elements that reflect their accountabilities. In Canada, that has meant, in a fashion utterly indicative of our multinational history, demographics and geography, that federalism was not simply optional for the shaping of a Canadian body politic, but in reality, the only option.

Federalism was the critical means by which conflicting interests were reconciled and the potential for future conflicts managed through a system of smaller units, pooling some powers in the centre while leaving vital powers with the pre-Confederation local governments. Without that confederal trade-off between what remains decentralized and what is placed in the central administration's purview, there would have been no Canada.

It remains the critical attraction of federalism in contemporary times. As Ron Watts, one of the world's most eminent scholars in comparative federalism recently pointed out:

> ...more and more peoples have come to see some form of federalism, combining a shared government for specified common purposes with autonomous action by constitutional units of government for purposes related to maintaining their regional distinctiveness as allowing the

closest institutional approximation to the multi-national
reality of the contemporary world (Watts 1999: 4).

This balance with respect to where powers of government are exercised is fundamental to the way Canada came
together in the 19th century and remains viable in the 21st
century and beyond.

Clearly, the role of federalism as a manager of conflicting interests, as the critical instrument for reconciling local
and geopolitical differences across the country was key to
the creation and survival of Canada itself. At the same time,
that central and ongoing dynamic role should absolutely
make us all very, very wary of efforts to impose new overarching institutions or powers that dilute the decentralized
character of Canada as a federation where, as a defining
characteristic, there is at least as much explicit paramoutcy
between jurisdictions in designated areas under the Constitution—areas vital to facilitating how Canada itself was
founded, as to anything else.

And whatever the case one might make, not without
justification for strong national institutions, it is vital not
to assume that national programs and federal government
institutions are one and the same. To accept that the definition of 'national' would be, at a stroke, to deny the extent
to which clearly compelling 'national' realities, like health
insurance, car licence portability, the administration of justice under one criminal code, the way financial institutions
like banks, credit unions, co-ops, trust companies and insurance enterprises, are actually governed and environmental
protection or health and safety inspections really transpire.
All are made real by different levels of government discharg-
ing their respective jurisdictions under Sections 91 and 92 of
the Canadian Constitution.

And while various assessments of the pre-Confederation
debates accurately represent what the different views were,
at the time of the polemic between centralized and decentralized organizational options, the hard truth of the final
core agreement is undeniable. Perhaps the most prominent
of Quebec's premiers put it clearly and succinctly:

...Confederation is made of provincial authorities within the scope of their jurisdiction and a sovereign central authority within the scope of its jurisdiction. When Confederation was discussed and decided upon, it was based on the principle of complete provincial autonomy (Duplessis 1950: 7).

Duplessis' view has prevailed for all subsequent Quebec premiers, of all political affiliations. This never however, stood in the way of decentralized authorities or the provinces working together with provincial counterparts to achieve appropriate national goals around issues like portability.

The reason that an amalgam of provincial and federal, or decentralized and centralized, can produce what is truly 'national' more efficiently than the federal government on its own, even with endless pots of money, is in no way unclear. The reason is the vital capacity of federalism and decentralized powers within a constitution to manage and maximize the benefits of diversity.

Diversity is not only a good thing. In its complexity, it can be about barriers to effective program design and delivery that can frustrate even the most compelling of public policy goals. As Canada becomes more multi-ethnic and pluralist over time, as the core duality of the English-French foundational confederal structure is called upon to shoulder more and more diversity pressures, federalism becomes even more vital for the future than it has been in the past. And the most vital portion of the confederal agreement remains the tolerance for, and embrace of, a dynamic decentralized view of how policy, programs, social and civil infrastructure are made relevant at street level in Canada's different regions and provinces.

The safety valve of subsidiarity

One need not be in the grips of a numbing global leverage and credit meltdown, in which Canada and Canadians in provinces as different as Prince Edward Island and British

Columbia are victimized in their local communities by forces that were initiated beyond our shores, jurisdictions or regulatory capacity, to understand why local decision making is a good thing. But it does help focus the mind.

One of the realities of international trade flows, external pressures on currencies and the apparent capacity of communication and digital technologies to penetrate and bring down all barriers and obliterate local difference, is that for all the good they generate in terms of poverty reduction for literally hundreds of millions of our fellow human beings in India and China and elsewhere, they can quite unwittingly be deeply destructive of any local sense of efficacy, coherence or security, economic or cultural.

For better or for worse, providing some protection for local identity, demographic and economic sustainability is at the core of the Canadian bargain and the confederal promise. In a world where stripping local and historically consequential and geographically contained populations of meaningful self-government or related and legitimate measures of control over vital aspects of their own way of life, neighborhoods or local civil, social and hard infrastructure has usually been seen as an attack upon identity and rights, protecting the decentralized aspect of our federation has never mattered more.

A society's coherence, embrace of common values and capacity for economic and social resilience is rarely the product of edicts or declarations from centrally focused elites—either bureaucratic, business or media. The latter groups usually simply reflect a mix of existing value expressions as filtered by the elites' own self-interest or perception of public interest. It is how effective, fulfilled, safe, secure and competent people feel in their own homes, communities or provinces that determines a country's sense of potential or opportunity. The local reality may be part of a larger political, economic or social reality—nationwide or globally. But if that reality is not 'right', it is the only reality that ultimately matters.

The subsidiarity principle, that the level of government closest to the population being served by any program or policy should be administering it, is not only about competent local knowledge for program design or delivery, as if that were not enough. It is also about accountability between those being served, the citizens to whom government reports and those charged with delivering the service as well as those to whom they report.

The more subsidiarity is unnecessarily diluted between different levels of government who are reporting via different levels to different places, the more the democratic notion of accountability is itself, diluted and weakened. That weakening and dilution feeds the cynicism about government and about a society's capacity to make progress together; it diminishes the potential in all levels of government and exacerbates legitimacy challenges and concerns. This is one of the most serious risks associated with any effort to halt progress towards greater subsidiarity in favour of greater centralization—a trend that when spotted should be assaulted as quickly as possible.

Subsidiarity is a safety valve within any large governance structure, regional or national. It is a way of ensuring that local sensitivities and potential tensions are addressed in program design, delivery and administration before those sensitivities become deeply counterproductive.

We can look at a series of federal programs such as the long gun registry, mid-1990 cuts to employment insurance eligibility, Wheat Board rigidity, to name three recent examples, where the absence of genuine subsidiarity became solid political and program problems. For federal systems, diluting subsidiarity threatens the areas of consensus and cooperative engagement between regions, peoples, geographies, cultures, languages and economies that are collectively vital to the economic and political viability of the country as a whole.

Those who seek to dilute subsidiarity or frustrate its progress over time, however well intentioned, are, in the context of the underlying tensions and competing aspirations within any federation (especially Canada), playing an extremely risky game. And the *de facto* entanglement of federal taxation powers, through conditional or unconditional funding of provincial programs, has produced remarkable obfuscation of exactly who is responsible for what. We have reached a point where blaming another level of government for problems in services for which the provinces have clear jurisdiction is the common political narrative. This dilutes the actual purpose of both democratic politics and debate federally or provincially, and has helped contribute to declining voter turnout at both levels. And the historic ability of the federal government to launch federal programs that build provincial client bases, whether jointly financed by the province or totally by Ottawa, and then at times of federal fiscal crisis capriciously end them leaving provinces in the lurch, is consistent. It may, in fact, be the most consistent part of federal fiscal policy and, by definition, the most harmful to subsidiarity and the integrity of the federal–provincial balance.

It was Tom Courchene who, amongst many others, pointed out how Ottawa put its "fiscal house in order" on the "fiscal backs of the provinces" (Courchene 2002: 33). That particular 1995 budgetary measure trimmed six billion dollars from the transfers to provinces. Previous decisions in the fiscal-crisis years of the Conservatives to end cost-sharing on the Canada Assistance Plan at the precise time that the recession of the early 1990s was increasing welfare costs in the provinces, also ranks as an unconstructive destabilization of any sense of partnership, and a negative factor relative to the viability of subsidiarity.

This kind of action does more than destabilize important social pillars like health services, education and welfare. It also fuels the case for those who argue, at the very least, for more disentanglement, at the very most, for a process of de-federalization, or complete separation.

Program learning: from the bottom up

Even the most determined proponent of the role of the federal government within Confederation, would surely have to accept that the Ottawa mandarin mindset cannot be all-knowing or consistently sensitive to local needs or differences. Whomever Canadians send to Ottawa to defend their local interests and advance the national interest must face off head to head with the federal public service.

Despite the thousands of hard working, patriotic, skilled, diligent and publicly-spirited public servants we are all fortunate to have in our employ, the federal public service is about the federal government first, its institutions, pre-rogatives, fiscal pools and administrative discretion and their protection. The statutes that govern their departmen-tal activity, the highly centralized nature of its structure and choking hierarchy, and the Auditor-General psychosis (which is not the Auditor General's fault, but the fault of the way in which senior departmental managers and deputies make risk-aversion more important than results), make it very hard and very risky indeed for public servants to think nationally as opposed to federally. They are about 'their government', 'their programs', 'their administrative proce-dures and manual of administration'.

What this produces, of course, is a barrier to learning, change, risk-taking and innovation in anything but the most superficial and self-centred of ways. I do not for one moment believe this to be the explicit intent of the senior public ser-vice. Indeed, many compelling leaders in the public service would protest vigorously to the contrary. But they would be, in some cases, so entrapped in the bubble of self-rever-ence that suffocates large parts of official Ottawa, that their normative bearings have simply been lost in the midst.

Hard working MPs spend large amounts of time plead-ing for programs to be more locally sensitive or embracing of local reality—as the Treasury Board system, Privy Coun-cil Office and departmental senior management urge 'Min-isters du jour' to hold the line. The debate between fairness and sensitivity, consistency versus increased local options is a daily part of the frustrating focus on process that paralyses Ottawa and slows its apprehensive or reactive acuity. This endless tug-of-war sustains those on the Left who argue that Ottawa is too focused on macro-forces to be meaning-ful in the local lives of different regions or address disparate regional or provincial needs, and fuels those on the Right who attack the entire premise of government overall being able to be a positive force. While both criticisms are over-blown, they help energize a sense of federal detachment from reality on the ground.

What this means in terms of learning, ongoing quality improvement, citizen-focused government and regional sensitivity, is that Ottawa is limited by the above constraints from being the source of much or any of what is required. From fiscal to health policy, from child care to post-second-ary education, from the environment to transportation, Ottawa serves best when it allows its decisions to be shaped by learning that takes place in local and provincial jurisdic-tions. The issue here is not the inter-provincial operation of matters under Section 91 of the Constitution. The issue is what happens when Ottawa engages in federal spending power activities that, by definition, relate to existing pro-vincial areas of Section 92 jurisdiction.

A classic example of this is in the endless dialectic on child care and early childhood education. If the purport and weight of the terms used in Sections 91 and 92 mean anything at all, this is clearly an area of explicit provin-cial jurisdiction and, at the very least, almost exclusionary dominance. Ottawa's efforts in the Martin administration years, to cobble together a series of federal-provincial con-tracts that would, in the end, influence provinces to essen-tially replicate Quebec's *garderies à cinq dollars* or five dollar a day daycare, spoke eloquently to the federal government's self-obsession. After unceremoniously slashing the social transfers to the provinces by one third, as part of what was an admittedly difficult fiscal challenge in the mid 1990s, Ottawa had diminished not only the provincial capacity to innovate, but their very capacity to maintain vital pillars of health care, education and welfare. Quebec made daycare a priority nonetheless. And while there are econometric and social criticisms of their program design, it was a step ahead and one quite responsive to the mood of Quebecers on the issue and related policy challenge.

Rather than simply assume that the *Federal-Provincial Relations Act* and fiscal practice ensured provincial capacity to address its Section 92 obligations and address the fiscal imbalance the 1990s had produced—undermining fiscal capacity in the provinces—Ottawa sought to create a boutique federal program and use contractual agreements to impose a jurisdiction it did not have. Whatever the strengths or weaknesses of the subsequent government's approach to the problem in terms of a universal indexed monthly grant for all children under six, and there are strong views on both sides of the ledger, the Harper government was operating within its own jurisdiction.

Quebec has learned from what its program does well and can do better, and can and has made changes to accommodate what has been learned. And, as a province, it has engaged in innovative joint programs with not-for-profit foundations to focus on the early years in terms of nutrition, health, exercise, learning and poverty beyond the existent day care program. There is no reason to believe that other provinces would not do the same. But when faced with an option of giving the provinces their full fiscal capacity to make choices on their own, or being less than adequate in terms of unconditional transfers, and trying to design and then impose boutique programs upon the provinces, official and political Ottawa took the latter course.

And that would be because federal tax receipts (which are gathered from residents, businesses and economic sectors in the provinces) are viewed in Ottawa as 'Ottawa's money/Ottawa's federal spending capacity'. This produces the bubble effect that causes real difficulty to innovation and citizen-focused programs. It also, of course, only deepens federal aspirations in normal economic times to 'hoover up' as much as possible in spending capacity for Ottawa's use—leaving the option of taxing less, or redistributing tax points to encourage more sensitive and effective subsidiarity off any meaningful discussion agenda when Privy Council Office or Finance Canada officials are in the room (which means off any meaningful discussion agendas *writ* large).

Decentralization, innovation and best practices

Canadians owe Saskatchewan and those who have engaged in public life and policy work from Saskatchewan more than can likely ever be repaid. The crisp nature of debates on everything from health care to federal-provincial fiscal planning to agriculture, to energy resources and royalties, to First Nations, to higher education and science and technology is never without a Saskatchewan perspective which is usually broader than just Saskatchewan's interests. But an exchange between two prominent Saskatchewan voices around health care in recent years is of profound purport to any effort to understand the compelling value of a decentralized federation.

The recent Royal Commission on the Future of Health Care in Canada (the Romanow Report) made a strong case for the existing system, with some modest innovation and a lot more money. Many who admire and admired the Hon. Roy John Romanow had hoped that he would bell the cat on shibboleths about our health care programs and insurance structure that desperately required being addressed. The report had many useful and thoughtful areas of research and study, and substantive insights of real value. But a clarion call for systemic change it was not.

When asked about the need to experiment with new approaches, such as more private sector service delivery under the public universal insurance model, Romanow very much left the impression that the nature of the system had been decided decades ago and system-transforming or challenging experimentation would not be of any great value.

Tom Courchene, a Senior Scholar at the Institute for Research on Public Policy, and Professor of Economics at the School of Policy Studies at Queen's University, asked what would have happened to the prospects for Medicare in the Canada of the 1960s, if the then Premier of Saskatchewan, the Hon. Tommy Douglas, had taken the same view as Romanow had taken in his Royal Commission on Health Care.

This question underlines the facility for innovation, new departures, policy experimentation and new analytical paradigms at the local level that would be utterly excluded from reality in Ottawa by the multi-layered, process-driven, fiscal obsession of the federal government. We have Medicare today because one province had the courage to innovate, face the difficult political waters of so doing, and two federal governments, the Rt. Hon. John Diefenbaker's and the Rt. Hon. Lester B. Pearson's, decided to commission and act on the findings of a study on what Saskatchewan's innovation meant for Canada (The Hall Report, commissioned by Diefenbaker and reported into the Pearson government). This is demonstrably how change happens in Canada.

Ontario's Guaranteed Annual Income Supplement for Seniors (GAINS), brought in under the Davis administration in the late 1970s, became the model for Ottawa and the other provinces, and the first serious step in overcoming poverty among the aged. Imagine where we would be if Ontario had lacked the fiscal capacity to finance this kind of innovation. Imagine where Canadians would be if Saskatchewan could not have innovated in the way it did. We know that changing technologies, demographic shifts, migration patterns, climate change, an aging population and what is likely to be a radically altered mix of economic models after this deep recession has run its course are likely to make public policy a more challenging and change-acute field.

Subsidiarity and decentralization are vital scouting posts through which to anticipate change, read it at ground level with all its ramifications and nuances, and shape policies that can, if not stay ahead of the curve, at the very least see where the curve is headed, and keep programs and policies that are aimed at serving efficiently and humanely from heading off a cliff. And while macro-trends in technology and global economic flows will be larger than Canada and any of her regions or provinces, facilitating local adaptability, ensuring sustainability and securing the right balance between economic expansion and social progress are vital to keeping Canada and Canadians in the game, while they are given the chance to build lives for themselves and their families that are sustained by equality of opportunity.

That will actually mean different things at various levels in First Nations communities, southern BC, Northern Ontario and Cape Breton. The nuances of the Beauce and Montreal will be different from those in Sudbury or downtown Toronto or Calgary. That very diversity for Canada and its people is a compelling economic and geopolitical strength. Just as a physician must first ensure that he or she does no harm, so too must the federal government ensure that it does not make this apprehensive and pro-active adaptability any harder for the provinces or Canadians in general.

Federal spending power: containing the threat

Open federalism of the present government appears to be a more pragmatic approach to respecting Sections 91 and 92 of the Constitution. Addressing the spending power is a vital priority—and was referenced in the Throne Speech of 2007:

> Our government believes that the constitutional jurisdiction of each order of government should be respected. To this end, guided by our federalism of openness, our Government will introduce legislation to place formal limits on the use of the federal spending power for new shared-cost programs in areas of exclusive provincial jurisdiction. This legislation will allow provinces and territories to opt out with reasonable compensation if they offer compatible programs (Canada 2007).

The Fathers of Confederation knew of what they spoke when they framed Sections 91 and 92 of the *British North America Act*. The drift by Ottawa to greater use of the spending power has become a larger irritant, especially when, as was the case with the Millennium Scholarship initiative Ottawa was so eager to launch, it essentially ignored provincial financial assistance laws for post-secondary students.

The hard truth about the spending power, when used by Ottawa, is that results of federal governments of all affiliations using the spending power specifically for boutique federal programs have been at best spotty and at worst calamitous. We can make any list you want—but if it includes shared cost health programming which the Hon. Marc Lalonde in 1974 nailed for producing perverse incentives, the real progress (or lack of same) on poverty, based on both direct account and shared cost or transfer programming, the management of First Nations' policies or the adaptability of health care to demographic change, the actual record is less than compelling.

Decisions over the spending power, its use and constraint have been part of most constitutional tensions and debates for over half a century. Generally, Canada's Liberal party has been a proponent of its use, claiming it as a vital instrument for sustaining national citizenship-related social policy or related goals. They have often received support in this from the so-called 'have-not provinces'.

Canada's Conservative leadership have been more anxious about the top-down constitutionally and confederally disruptive nature of the spending power and have sought, from the days of the Meech Lake Accord in 1987 to the Charlottetown Accord of 1992, to the Throne Speech of 2007, to constrain its use, allowing opting out by the provinces with compensation. To be fair to the Rt. Hon. Jean Chrétien's Liberal administration, the Social Union Framework Accord, signed in February of 1999 by all provinces save Quebec, did try and provide some protection relative to federal spending power decisions on social policy areas clearly within provincial jurisdiction.

The tension that the use of the spending power exacerbates runs to the core of every Quebec premiers' concern about the binary code of Confederation as an agreement that liberated Quebec from the minority-swamping dynamic of the old Province of Canada in favour of provincial autonomy as defined by Section 92 of the *British North America Act*.

Every time a federal government uses the spending power, it negates the core premise of Confederation and, willy nilly, encourages those forces in Quebec who argue Confederation is unworkable. And while no doubt well-intentioned, willful and capricious use of the spending power implies that only Ottawa can respond to social or other needs, and that Ottawa responding is a better option than having provinces with appropriate and robust fiscal capacity responding on their own, on terms that make sense locally.

It is a concept that positions the provinces not as partners with their own areas of clear sovereignty—especially on social programs as provided for in Section 92—but as subsidiaries always held captive by the policy preferences of the federal government of the day. While the case has and will be made that this is, from time to time, necessary, that case eats away at the foundations of Confederation itself with corrosive effect. In fact, much of the negotiations around the so-called 'Social Union Accord' was about finding a way to put some measure of control around the capriciousness on the use of the spending power by Ottawa because of the destabilizing effect of that very caprice. As one of the scholars who analyzed the process that led to the accord observed:

> ... with its spending power, Ottawa can unilaterally launch spending initiatives based on shared cost programs that it has fully financed, or direct payments to individuals or institutions in areas that are entirely within provincial jurisdiction. Left without judicial supervision, the spending power means that the federal government can unilaterally change to its advantage the Canadian Constitution, especially to ensure its own visibility (Tremblay 2000: 156).

This judicially unsupervised interest is made even more daunting when one understands that Canada's final arbiter of federal-provincial disputes, the Supreme Court of Canada, is appointed exclusively by the federal government. Other federations have their federal constitutional courts appointed by both levels of government. The regional or provincial rights' role, sometimes assigned to the Senate of Canada, is also made more difficult by the hard truth that the federal Prime Minister has had, since Confederation, the exclusive individual right to make recommendations to the Crown (which are always accepted) for appointments to this body.

And, before someone tried to do something on the fiscal disequilibrium—which the governments that preceded the Rt. Hon. Stephen Harper's simply denied existed—the pro-file of the spending power looked like this: Ottawa would slash transfers to the provinces in the mid 1990s by about a third, starting a trend of health care, post-secondary and social service cutbacks from which we have yet to recover. Ottawa would raise its taxes. The provinces would be forced to re-profile their priorities to deal with Ottawa's cutbacks. In Ontario alone, but not uniquely, health care spending has gone up 20 percent and real expenditures on post-sec-ondary education have declined by at least as much. Some provinces sought to cut taxes to help their industrial and productive sectors survive under the federal tax assault.

Free trade, the GST and economic recovery fattened Ottawa coffers in a way that saw deficits turn quickly into surpluses. These surpluses should have spoken directly to reducing taxes or transferring tax points to the provinces. Instead, they produced a plethora of new 'pre-endowed' federal foundations or bodies and newly designed bou-tique federal programs. This reflects the core bias of 'the money is ours' which permeates the federal bureaucracy and especially Finance Canada and the 'Ottawa knows best' bias which the federal Liberals and New Democrats usu-ally share with the federal public service. Ottawa did all this management of the surplus while most of the provinces were struggling.

Throughout both the deficit period that began in 1973 and the massive surplus period that began around 1996, the federal Finance Department was always consistent—it did not once, within plus or minus ten percent, predict the surplus or the deficit accurately. The federal spending power indeed!

So, the mood among Big C (Conservatives) and small c (conservatives) was that the more money that is afforded the provinces for their legitimate fiscal and social obligations and the more money one can responsibly leave in taxpayers hands, the more balanced and productive all aspects of our social and economic framework will be.

The dynamics of 'open federalism' will depend in part, on how Finance Canada will choose to interpret the government's commitment or what they and their colleagues at Treasury Board Secretariat or Privy Council Office will do to try and conserve Ottawa's fiscal capacity. Culturally, it is completely understandable that having seen the land of deep and destructive deficits and the land of billions of dollars in surplus, the public service, who live and work in Ottawa, would prefer the latter context. The fact that some fiscal disequilibrium dollars were distributed to the provinces in the Hon. James Flaherty's first budget, some health care money and reinvestment took place under both the Rt. Hon. Paul Martin and the Rt. Hon. Stephen Harper are huge moral victories, not to mention the GST cuts. But this has gone against Finance Canada's core and perpetual strategy of fiscal self-preservation.

The struggle for a straightened and formally constrained spending power will be a difficult one. While the vast majority of health care, education and social service funding comes from the provinces, lobby groups, the federal bureaucracy and scholars with solid methodology and genuine concern will push to enhance Ottawa's fiscal capacity and spending initiative at the expense of the taxpayer and the provinces. They are a powerful force—as they have every right to be in a democracy—and they will be no doubt sustained by the bureaucracy itself in the many ways a bureaucracy can.

This debate engages of course, the trajectory very much before us on equalization itself. The fact that Ontario may qualify briefly—and that Newfoundland will be making fiscal progress with an unemployment rate now just down to 13 percent, should be untroubling. There is no injustice in this temporary relative ratio any greater than the core injustice to the 12–14 percent of Canadians who remain beneath the low income cut off in this country—a number that is worse in rural Canada, and a number that is immeasurably worse among our First Nations people and single parents.

Equalization is a relative gauge of per capita spending power in specific areas of the country. When oil prices exceeded US$ 120 a barrel for a time, it is no failure of policy that relative balance mechanisms appeared temporarily out of whack. If equalization is relative, the spending power and Sections 91 and 92 of the Constitution are not. They are core definitions of how we balance the federation and let provinces have the fiscal sovereignty and program initiative in areas that are primarily their jurisdiction.

While the fact that the pre-Confederation negotiations at Quebec City and Charlottetown spent far less time on the division of powers than was spent on the role and qualifications of the Senate is troubling, there was a rationale to the division of powers then and it holds now. We need always to remember that the core purpose of a federation and the division of power is the intrinsic management of potentially corrosive differences and interests: "The function of federations is not to eliminate internal differences, but rather to preserve regional identities within a united framework. Their function is not to eliminate conflict but to manage it in such a way that regional differences are accommodated" (Watts 1999: 110–111). Then, it was rural societies that wanted things managed in local ways by people directly accountable to them—with only those issues like the currency, weights and measures, defence, the criminal law and related issues that defined a pan-provincial interest set by Ottawa. With the Statute of Westminster in 1931, foreign policy became more real and a large part, with defence, of the intrinsic Ottawa role.

Today, the pressures of globalization and market linkage and the train wrecks that can pile on quickly when something like the American financial framework fails, argue not only for an Ottawa strong, competent and well-resourced in its own jurisdictions, but also for provinces able to discharge their own obligations within their jurisdictions with appropriate resources. This argues against the use of the spending power in areas outside the explicit and defined realities of

Section 91, certainly during non-emergency times of peace. It argues for Ottawa facilitating a tax and transfer regime that leaves as much money as possible in the provinces' hands and those of the taxpayers.

Solutions to health care restructuring and post-secondary financing going forward are to be found in the provincial domain and more market friendly sensitivity. Ottawa's treasury is not the source of solutions here—but can be, if improperly deployed, the source of frustration, misdirection and solutions lost or delayed.

Equalization transfers wealth between rich governments and poor governments—not among rich and poor people. *In extremis*, equalization can be a disincentive to labour mobility and economic efficiency.

Within its own jurisdiction, Ottawa could move on poverty through a negative income tax. It is the ultimate way the federal government could contribute to productivity— reduce poverty, which is the most serious of public health negative determinants, promote efficiency and express its 'peace and good government' mission. It would allow provinces to shift much of the welfare spending into education—which is a much better way to produce good health outcomes—and allow Ottawa over time, to re-structure transfer programs in support of a national commitment to end poverty, while leaving provincial jurisdictions intact.

In due course, this would be efficient, validate the federal government across Canada, reduce provincial spending burdens that are fixed and can be done through the federal tax system.

Being strong at what it should do: a federal option

This essay does not diminish the intensity of the debate between Right and Left, business and labour, east and west, 'have' and 'have not' provinces as to how broad the federal government's reach might best be in the perpetual future. This debate lies at the root of our federal/provincial debates, our First Ministers' Conferences and the defining politics between the four parliamentary parties.

Obviously, at one extreme, we would find a Parti Québécois Quebec government supported by their Bloc Québécois allies in the federal House of Commons who would, in so far as Quebec is concerned, see no role whatever for the Government of Canada (except for sending money). At the opposite end of the spectrum, we would find some Atlantic provinces, some determined advocates for social policy intervention and others who distrust provincial nuance and prerogative, make the case for a more robust federal role.

Advocates for the greater fiscal sovereignty of the large cities, of which there are many who are well-informed, well-organized and well-intentioned, would see an Ottawa–provincial balance reformed to accept the cities as almost equal fiscal partners. This debate will define much of our jurisdictional and substantive political discussion for many decades to come.

The case for robust decentralization and well-provisioned subsidiarity is not fashioned on the premise of federal impotence or weakness—quite to the contrary. A federal government that was robust within its own federal jurisdiction and able to discharge its Constitutional mandates around monetary policy, defence, foreign affairs, First Nations, energy, fiscal re-distribution, national policing for a federal criminal code, national security, border management, modernization and other precisely federal institutions and obligations, rather than one that underperforms in many of these areas (notwithstanding which party is in power) because its resources are dissipated across too broad a spectrum of activities (many of which would be best done and more adroitly delivered and provided at the provincial level)—would be broadly welcomed. Moreover, the destructive effect of having a military that is under-resourced, a federal diplomatic core that is too small for the tasks at hand, a national police force whose training and effectiveness is financially constrained or a public broadcaster that is proven to be, among the other tier 1 broadcasters internationally, massively under-funded on a per capita basis, only diminishes the standing and relevance of any federal government under any political party. This is compounded by unwelcome and poorly executed federal spending power excursions that disrupt provincial jurisdiction and are seen as politically motivated without either predictability or dependability.

The consistent use by Ottawa, for example, of 'conditionality' on federal transfers or social programs has had a constraining and negative effect on the kind of progressive and responsive social policy conditions required. Provinces have complained about the negative impact conditionality imposes on the freedom they need to adapt to street-level social conditions.

> One legitimate claim of the provinces is that conditionality tends to limit the scope for experimentation and innovation in programme design and therefore their ability to respond to new circumstances.... ... it is an undesirable aspect of conditional grant programmes that they do not allow provinces sufficient flexibility in programme design (Hobson and St-Hilaire 1994: 63).

Conditionality on transfers is clearly fiscal overreach and usually produces distortions or perverse outcomes—without strengthening the federation.

Smart and effective federal government is a far cry from large, overreaching, 'jurisdiction-blurring', centralizing governments that have neither the resources nor acuity to achieve effectively what they take upon themselves. And when they do this in a way that dilutes either taxpayer liquidity or the capacity of provincial governments to meet their own Section 92 responsibilities, they actually do venture into the range of the 'doing harm' context that needs to be avoided at all cost.

There are examples of mishaps at both ends of the spectrum. Quebec's handling of labour training and skills development after that part of the old 'manpower' federal mandate was downloaded in the 1990s will be a case study in inefficient and ineffective devolution for decades to come. Ottawa's *de facto* usurping of provincial resource rights through the use of the federal taxation power under the Rt. Hon. Pierre Trudeau and the Hon. Marc Lalonde in the 1970s National Energy Program continues to drive wedge politics in the west and seed the clouds with provincial and private sector suspicion of Ottawa. There can be excesses on both sides. But the issue going forward is what Ottawa's role, as defined by the Constitution, means in the years and decades ahead, and how provinces can meet their obligations with the fiscal capacity vital for that task. This is often portrayed by one political party as a question of national unity and what it means to be a Canadian citizen—and I am sure this view is both sincerely held by those who prefer a centralist option and those who embrace the defining role of innovations like the Charter of Rights and Freedoms in 1983. Liberals often portray themselves as the party of the Charter which they certainly are—notwithstanding the help they received from Premiers like the Hon. William Davis in Ontario and the Hon. Richard Hatfield in New Brunswick—and have every right to do. Historically, Conservatives have been more interested in the actual contents of Sections 91 and 92 and the legitimate and clear roles both sections described for each level of government. Those sections run to the core understanding at the root of Confederation.

The way ahead

There are a host of issues facing Canada that require leadership from different levels of government. Rapid solutions that radically decentralize, or centralize would make little constructive sense relative to critical issues like national security—in which, for example, while Ottawa has a crucial and dominant role, we are also utterly dependant in terms of local capacity of first responders on police, fire and health care services within provincial jurisdiction. Poverty, where provincial welfare programs have had no effect in reducing the absolute number of people living under the poverty line or the percentage overall of Canadians trapped in poverty, including many who hold down more than one job, is another area where there is no limit to the kind of creativity that can ensue, especially if local and federal jurisdictions are respected. An Ottawa focused on its redistributive and national taxing role could reduce the number of Canadians living beneath the poverty line. Innovation at the local field could be enhanced and deepened if the core burden of lifting people out of monetary poverty were addressed by the federal government without serious program design burdens.

A federal government that continues to tax away provincial fiscal jurisdictional capacity is not one anticipated by those who replaced the Martin administration, which, to its credit, had also begun to modestly re-invest in unconditional transfers. But the Harper Conservatives, who have taken the positive step of investing billions in fiscal equilibrium for the provinces, and in substantial tax cuts, have been slowed in their progress by a federal bureaucracy and Finance Department that see federal revenues as rightly Ottawa's and would rather collect too much and keep its allocation prerogatives undiminished going forward year by year than allow a gradual structural change that actually increased provincial capacity for program design, local innovation and the full promise of creative and engaged decentralization. Some day, some government and Parliament will have to confront this radical centralist bias that, if left unchecked, will suffocate the brilliance of Confederation, dilute the ultimate promise of federalism and weaken Canada and its prospects unnecessarily but assuredly in the process.

The genius of Confederation and the *British North America Act* was in the balance between Ottawa and the founding constituent provinces which created the federal government to begin with. That balance has been tilted by the federal government and fiscal flows away from the Section 92 responsibilities of the provinces and the legitimate fiscal tools they need to do the job. We would be better advised to pursue a path of establishing clarity in the roles of different levels of government and ensuring the transfer of tax points, bolstered by equalization if necessary, to the provinces so that they can effectively discharge their Section 92 roles.

As a distinguished Canadian scholar observed, while comparing British devolution under the Rt. Hon. Tony Blair and our own federal-provincial balance: "In Canada we need to clarify roles, responsibilities and lines of account- ability and increase transparency... And we need to find better ways to involve legislatures in monitoring and debat- ing inter-jurisdiction issues..." (Simeon 1999: 60).

Maintaining the balance and tilting toward the opportu- nities of decentralization while resisting undue 'federaliza- tion' of fiscal or instrumental options is a vital component of moving Canada forward. Letting that balance dissipate and diluting the mix between centralization and decentraliza- tion that *ab initio* favoured the decentralization tilt would diminish Canadian federalism—and perhaps Canada itself, its creativity and its resilience going forward.

References

Canada 2007. Office of the Prime Minister (October 16). *Speech from the Throne*. www.pmo.gc.ca [consulted March 23, 2010].

Courchene, Thomas J. 2002 (July). "Half Way Home: Canada's Remarkable Fiscal Turnaround and the Paul Martin Legacy." *Policy Matters*, 3: 8: 33.

Duplessis, Maurice 1950. "Secrétariat aux affaires inter-gouvernentales canadiennes, Quebec's Historical Position of the Federal Spending Power–1944-1988." Opening speech at the Dominion-Provincial Conference, January 10, Ottawa.

Hobson, Paul and France St. Hilaire 1994. *Federal Provincial Fiscal Arrangements: Toward Sustainable Federalism*. Montreal: Institute for Research on Public Policy.

Romanow, Hon. Roy John 2002 (November). *Building on Values: The Future of Health Care in Canada*. Ottawa: Privy Council Office. www.publica- tions.gc.ca [consulted March 23, 2010].

Simeon, Richard 1999. *In the Dynamics of Decentralization*. Montreal and Kingston, ON: McGill-Queen's University Press.

Tremblay, André 2000. *Federal Spending Power in the Canadian Social Union without Quebec*. Montreal: Institute for Research on Public Policy, McGill University.

Watts, Ronald 1999. *Comparing Federal Systems*. 2nd ed. Kingston: Institute of Intergovenmental Relations, Queen's University.

Chapter 5

Re-Federalizing Canada: Refocusing the Debate on Centralization

François Rocher
Marie-Christine Gilbert

Introduction

In both the academic literature and political discourse, the conventional wisdom holds that Canadian federalism is the most decentralized anywhere in the world. We wish to call this highly contestable proposition into question for two reasons. Firstly, it is based on a partial, fragmented and distorted concept of federalism that reveals the ideological biases of the authors and political actors with regard to their preferred concept of the Canadian political community rather than an understanding of a political regime that is supposed to be federal and that actually seeks to be so. Secondly, it seems evident to us that those who present Canadian federalism as either very or too decentralized base their arguments on shaky evidence that, after further analysis, appears very unconvincing to us.

In the first section of the chapter, we examine the ways in which federalism and decentralization ought to be seen as mutually reinforcing rather than as in opposition to one another. We offer a review of normative arguments that call for a more complex understanding of the federal reality. In particular, we follow Daniel Elazar, and before him Livingston, who pointed to the necessity of a federal culture: "The first step is a shift in the minds of men from thinking statist to thinking federal" (Elazar 1994: 12).

In this spirit, we contrast the monist and the pluralist approaches to federalism.

In the second section of the chapter, we demonstrate how the claims that Canadian federalism is very or too decentralized, and that it even constitutes the most decentralized regime in the world, rest on foundations that are, to say the least, very fragile. We begin by proposing working definitions of 'centralization' and 'decentralization' in order to underline the weaknesses of the arguments that present Canadian federalism as decentralized. We contend that, in fact, the workings of Canadian federalism show it to be a centralized system notably, but not exclusively, because of failures to respect the division of powers, the importance of the federal spending power, and the sometimes strong, often tenuous, constraints imposed through fiscal transfers and through administrative arrangements. We also contend that the decisions of the Supreme Court of Canada have reinforced this centralized reality over the years through the functional and institutional definitions of federalism that it has promoted by emphasizing the notion of efficiency. Still, the dominant view, repeated *ad nauseam,* holds that Canada is *de facto* decentralized on account of the increasing political capacity of the provinces. Having become more powerful, the provinces are depicted as an effective counterweight to the federal government. We will explain why this conclusion rests on a vague, if not impressionistic, assessment of the powers and relative autonomy of the provinces. Others arrive at this same conclusion. Their assessments however, are based on criteria such as the ratio of federal-provincial public spending, constitutional power, and the importance of the public service. As we will see, these indicators are also problematic.

In conclusion, we call for the necessity of 're-federalizing' the Canadian political system. In our view, certain avenues ought to be explored by, amongst other things, returning to the ideas of André Burelle who defended the principles of non-subordination, subsidiarity, and participation in the realization of common objectives. We do realize—as a dose of reality requires—that significant obstacles will have to be overcome along the road to re-federalization. Among these obstacles, it is important to note the absence of a federal culture in Canada and the hegemony of a monist concept of federalism in the public and academic spheres, as well as within the very structure of Canadian federalism itself.

On the purposes of federalism

In scholarly research, the practice of federalism can be analyzed as both a point of departure and of arrival. Federalism can also be understood in terms of a general philosophy of society, an institutional structure that embodies a specific concept of social relations amongst citizens and amongst constitutive communities. Some researchers distinguish federalism from federation. The latter refers to institutional arrangements based on an intra-state division of powers, while federalism, a much larger normative concept, speaks to a social ideal that federation is supposed to bring into being (Burgess 2006). It is important to recognize and preserve the diverse communities in the framework of the federation and to realize this initial objective by insisting upon specific institutional arrangements. In this sense, federalism is "a device through which differing nationalities could unite, and while retaining their own distinctive national existence, attempt to create in addition a new sense of common nationality" (Wheare 1996: 30).

It is also important to note that there is no single normative model of federalism. Instead, federalism is an idea, a principle, a phenomenon that is expressed in the practice and in the variety of existing federations (Théret 2005: 112). As a means of managing diversity, federalism calls for compromise and consensus to balance and reconcile seemingly contradictory fundamental principles. In this respect, federalism may be understood, in a 'pluralist' sense, as a form of political organization that aims to reconcile the principles of unity and diversity within a shared territory (Karmis and Norman 2005: 5).[1] Regardless of its historical roots and the way in which it has become politicized, social pluralism requires this flexible form of association in which centralized authority cannot and must not be absolute. Central authority must coexist with the autonomy of the federated entities. We will examine this principle of autonomy in greater detail later on.

All this being said, however, most studies of federalism, and *a fortiori* those that look at federalism in a comparative context, focus on the institutional workings of federations and assign very limited importance to the normative dimensions that animate them. If, as Lamontagne contends, a federation is always the product of a marriage of convenience and must be analyzed in terms of an instrumental rationality, no reflection upon the ethics of diversity management will be relevant to an assessment of the federal experience (Lamontagne 1954: 99). Furthermore, he adds, "within a federation, there are no absolute principles, merely different methods that must be employed or avoided according to their characteristics and to the requirements of the tasks to be accomplished" (Ibid.). From this perspective, reflection upon non-instrumental ends would be of little interest. But this conclusion is certainly debatable.

More recently, Bruno Théret rejected the existence of a normative model of federalism. Instead, he argues for the existence of an idea or a phenomenon that takes many forms. This argument is aimed less at denying the importance of reflecting on the federal principle as it is at critiquing the dominant tendency in the literature to consider the American model of federalism as an ideal (Théret 2005: 100). Théret does add that a federal system must be defined "as one in which a self-preservation mechanism is instituted for the federal principle which permanently regulates its constitutive contradiction between unity and diversity" (Ibid., 128). From this perspective, if unity overrides diversity or the reverse, if diversity triumphs at the expense of unity, one cannot speak of federalism (Ibid.).

In our opinion, there are practical consequences to taking account of the normative dimensions of federalism that are important to mention from the outset. As we have seen, the notion of federalism refers both to a set of institutions and to a set of principles that govern them. Consequently, federalism cannot be analyzed solely in terms of power structures; it also requires a detour along the road of ideas, representation, values and ideals. This perspective stands in opposition to a more instrumental view according to which federalism is considered to be nothing more than the sum total of calculated advantages and balances of power (Weinstock 2001). It is useful here to recall that the original Latin term *feodus* meant "union, pact, voluntary agreement or covenant," which assumes the existence of autonomous and equal individuals. At the root of the association, therefore, lies the principal of mutual consent, of cooperation, of partnership in pursuit of a common framework, all while preserving the integrity of the constituent entities. Consequently, a federal society is founded on recognition of pluralism and of the heterogeneity of the society itself. It allows that democracy can flourish in a political environment characterized by numerous and deep differences of opinion dividing the territorially-based social groups.

In contrast to unitary visions, social pluralism can give rise to a form of politics that rests on joint governance by minorities rather than on the principle of alternating majorities. What Arend Lijphart refers to as "democracy of pacification or consensus", and Elazar as "compounded majority", calls into question the notion that a unitary vision can be the only source of stability and social cohesion in a Westminster type democracy (Elazar 1982). In fact, federal democracy rejects the principle of simple majoritarianism, as the most important decisions are arrived at through collaborative mechanisms, be they official or not. Of course, a federal regime cannot have as its sole virtue the recognition of autonomous spaces for the federated entities (LeClair 2007: 66). It must also ensure a certain form of interdependence and collaboration.

It is important to recall that pluralist federalism suggests a model of governance that is open to asymmetries and plural identities, while also promoting conciliation between competing national initiatives (Cardinal and Brady 2007; Laforest 2008). It allows us to think of the modern nation-state in terms that extend beyond monistic and unitary sovereignty, to re-conceptualize the state in multinational terms that accord with the principle of autonomy. From this perspective, it could respond to the legitimate demands of Quebec and Aboriginal national initiatives by accommodating their differences both in the Constitution and in the operation of the federation.

Our remarks to this point have been made in general terms. It must be noted that every historical experience is unique and that there is no 'pure' or best federal structure or set of institutional characteristics that will produce a perfectly federal state. Therefore, we reject a 'checklist' approach to evaluating federal experiences and, *a fortiori*, the Canadian case. Nevertheless, it seems necessary to us to look back upon the intentions that underlay the decision to adopt a federal regime in Canada in the first place. The debate over whether our federal structure should be centralized or decentralized dealt with political objectives and with questions as to the political organization best suited to dealing with the nature of the tensions and the problems that had to be addressed as much as it did with a state-centred or non-state-centred assessment of the technical question of dividing powers. We contend that this latter element can only be made sense of in light of the common understandings that must have existed as to the intended definition of the Canadian political community.

Principles and practices of Canadian federalism

The concept of autonomy underpinning the federal system originates in the historical context of the emergence of the constitutional identity of the Canadian state. As André Burelle explains:

> ...it suffices to read the writings of Sir John A. Macdonald and George-Étienne Cartier in order to understand that, without the political necessity of providing the French

Canadians with a territory and the local powers required for the preservation of their language and culture, Canada would have been a unitary state rather than a federation (Burelle 2005: 402).[2]

The Judicial Committee of the Privy Council in London, the highest court of appeal in Canada until 1949, reiterated this notion several times. The most frequently cited example is in Liquidators of the Maritime Bank of Canada, which stated that:

The object of the Act was neither to weld the provinces into one, nor to subordinate provincial governments to a central authority, but to create a federal government in which they should all be represented, entrusted with the exclusive administration of affairs in which they had common interest, each province retaining its independence and autonomy. That object was accomplished by distributing, between the Dominion and the provinces, all powers executive and legislative, and all public property and revenues which had previously belonged to the provinces; so that the Dominion Government should be vested with such of these powers, property, and revenues as were necessary for the due performance of its constitutional functions and that the remainder should be retained by the provinces for the purposes of provincial government (Liquidators... 1892: 441–442; Adam 2008: 194).

The principle of autonomy that is attached to the Canadian federal principle must be understood not merely as provincial autonomy, but also in reference to a particular imperative. It originates in the general idea that, in a federal environment, each level of government must enjoy freedom of action in matters that fall within its exclusive jurisdiction (Brouillet 2004). In this sense, "the value of unity will be preserved if the federal level of government can exercise its legislative authority without major interference from the provincial governments, and vice versa, in keeping with the value of diversity" (Ibid., 129). On this point, James Tully, through the words of Judge Loranger, argues that:

...[i]n constituting themselves into a confederation, the provinces did not intend to renounce, and in fact never did renounce their autonomy. This autonomy with their rights, powers and prerogatives they expressly preserve for all that concerns their internal government (Tully 1995a: 141).

There is, therefore, no subordination to the federal government, but rather equality amongst the provinces. That being said, this idea is not universally accepted in Canada. The dominant perspective in the English-Canadian literature has expunged all references to the notion of autonomy, and instead emphasizes efficiency. In the works of francophone Quebec scholars, as well as in the governmental practices that are inspired by them, we find a more significant place accorded to this notion as well as to the idea of interdependence (Rocher 2009a; B. Pelletier 2001).[3] Furthermore, French-speaking writers have a tendency to take the provincialist thesis as the starting point for their discussions of federalism, whereas the centralist thesis remains at the heart of anglophone analyses (S. Kelly and Laforest 2004).

At the very heart of federalism, is the unavoidable issue of the division of powers, and the importance of the central and provincial governments each remaining within their respective spheres of coordinated and independent jurisdiction (Wheare 1963: 10). The combination of 'self-rule' and 'shared rule' (Elazar 1994: 21) can manage diversity, be it cultural, territorial or social, while at the same time preserving the unity of the political society governed by the state. In 1981, the Supreme Court of Canada's Resolution to Amend the Constitution reiterated this principle of unity, notably by urging the federal government to obtain the consent of a substantial number of provinces before carrying out the repatriation of the Constitution (Brouillet 2004: 12; Canada 1981, 1982). As Eugénie Brouillet describes it, "the Supreme Court considered the participation of both levels of government in the process of *constitutional amendment* to be necessary for the maintenance of the federal principle" (Brouillet 2004: 12, 14).[4] The Reference re: Secession of Quebec,

essentially reiterated the unity principle, but further emphasized recognition of the diversity of the constituents of the
Confederation and the means at the disposal of the provincial governments to ensure the development in their own
societies within their independent areas of jurisdiction. The
normative dimensions that hearken back to the objectives of
federalism are eloquently articulated in the following pas-
sage that is worth citing:

> The fundamental objectives of federalism were, and still
> are, to reconcile unity with diversity, promote democratic
> participation by reserving meaningful powers to the local
> or regional level and to foster co-operation among gov-
> ernments and legislatures for the common good. To attain
> these objectives, a certain degree of predictability with
> regard to the division of powers between Parliament and
> the provincial legislatures is essential. For this reason,
> the powers of each of these levels of government were
> enumerated in Ss. 91 and 92 of the Constitution Act, 1867
> or provided for elsewhere in that Act. As is true of any
> other part of our Constitution—this "living tree" as it is
> described in the famous image from Edwards v. Attorney-
> General for Canada, [1930] A.C. 124 (P.C.), at p. 136—the
> interpretation of these powers and of how they interrelate
> must evolve and must be tailored to the changing political
> and cultural realities of Canadian society. It is also impor-
> tant to note that the fundamental principles of our con-
> stitutional order, which include federalism, continue to
> guide the definition and application of the powers as well
> as their interplay. Thus, the very functioning of Canada's
> federal system must continually be reassessed in light of
> the fundamental values it was designed to serve (Adam
> 2008: 194).

In conclusion, whatever its constitutional structure, the
existence of every democratic state depends upon it achieving a balance amongst its constitutive elements. Two elements appear to characterize the Canadian federal balance:
the first, more formal element arises from the legal equality

between the orders of government, while the second more dynamic element is the product of the forces of centralization and decentralization, and includes, in particular, the distribution of resources and legislative powers (Ibid.).

Mis-understanding federalism

Analyses that emphasize centralization or de-centralization, which rest on this particular conception of federalism, focus above all on the division of powers and on how to protect the existence, integrity and authority of the respective governments (Watts 1999a: 36). In Quebec, the dominant interpretation further underlines the centralized character of the Founding Fathers' intentions and the fact that, given the subordination of the provinces to the federal government, federal practices have not respected the original spirit of the Constitution. The central government has neither sought to respect the principle of provincial autonomy, nor supported the participation of the provinces in decision making. In Quebec, the federal ideal resembles that of Frank Delmartino and Kris Deschouer who argue that "a federation is a political-institutional structure that offers its constitutive elements explicit guarantees of self-management over their own affairs and co-management over affairs of the state, thereby creating an equilibrium between the centre and the periphery appropriate to the proper conduct of public affairs" (Delmartino and Deschouer 1994: 14). In a union of this type, the federal and provincial governments should, in theory, act without the latter being subordinated to the former. The required balance is thus between the collective entities, between the federal state and the federated entities or amongst the federated entities themselves (Théret 2005: 112). This view was articulated in both the report of the Royal Commission of Inquiry on Constitutional Problems in 1956 (Quebec 1956: 209) and the report of the Commission on Fiscal Imbalance in 2002 (Seguin report), and it continues to be articulated to this day in Quebecois legal scholarship (Adam 2008: 40–41).[5]

Continuing on this subject, no analysis of the centralization arising from the organizational structure, specifically its judicial, institutional, administrative and political dimensions, can be complete without paying attention to the understanding of societal values inherent to pluralist federalism. For those engaged in the discourse of pluralism, for example: J. Tully, C. Taylor, W. Kymlicka, D. Karmis and W. Norman, the federal culture requires both a double loyalty and a shared identity.[6] The identity that is associated with the state in general, the integrator of the solidarities, is just as important as the reinforcement of collective autonomies. A corollary of the principal of autonomy, and of the division of powers that gives it political expression, is the idea that neither of the two orders of government can speak in the name of all of the citizens or of the entire political community. Neither the state as a whole, nor the federated states, can assert the exclusive right to represent the federal community. The division of powers, therefore, requires a double loyalty. The relationship between the orders of government is not competitive, but rather complementary. The ramifications of centralization are apparent in the development of the welfare state by the federal state that presents itself as the bearer of the subsumed and aggregated values of the majority. As Linda Cardinal and Marie-Joie Brady argue, the Romanow Commission on the Future of Health Care in Canada is a case in point. Its title, *Building on Values*, suggests that, in order to build a strong economy, Canadian values must guide government policy making in health care as well as in every other domain of public life (Cardinal and Brady 2007: 440). In fact, Canada is often "engaged in a vast enterprise of promoting its values and itself as a model for other societies to emulate" (Ibid.). This approach deviates from a concept of federalism that takes into account the necessary balance between common objectives and preserving the autonomy of the constituent units. As Carl Friedrich writes, "We can properly speak of federalism only if a set of political groupings coexist and interact as autonomous entities united in a common order with an autonomy of its own" (Friedrich 1974: 54). Any analysis that fails to take this into account will also fail to accurately describe Canadian federalism.

On whether the Canadian federation is centralized or decentralized

In order to determine the extent of centralization or decentralization in the Canadian political regime, we must understand these terms. At the level of politics or administration, 'centralization' is the uniting of diverse decision-making powers or powers of control in a single centre. In terms of the exercise of powers granted in whole or in part by the Constitution, there is 'centralization' when processes effectively concentrate the exercise of legislative and executive powers in the hands of the federal apparatus, whether or not this concentration was envisaged in the Constitution (B. Pelletier 2006). In other words, centralization increases the capacity of the central government to exercise its authority in areas of provincial jurisdiction, either through duly recognized transfers of power from the provinces to federal authorities, or through the implementation mechanisms that restrict planning, evaluation or control, to which the provinces are subordinate (Rocher and Rouillard 1996: 105). Decentralization can be understood conversely as the dynamic through which the central government can transfer a certain degree of its authority to the provinces. When this is accomplished through constitutional amendments, the devolution of power is irreversible. From a more global perspective, constitutionalists Henri Brun and Guy Tremblay make an interesting distinction in regards to the centre of power:

> When we say that a state is centralized, it is not always in reference to its administration. It could also be in regards to the whole power of the state, especially the supreme power, legislative sovereignty. Sovereignty is centralized when there is only one sovereign power centre in the state. By contrast, if we say that a state is decentralized, we mean that the legislative power is shared amongst several centres. The choice between centralization and decentralization becomes then a political question: it distinguishes unitary and federal states (Brun and Tremblay 2002: 403–407).

Decentralization can also occur through administrative agreements that result in unofficial delegations of power, either permanently or for a pre-determined temporary period of time (Ibid., 105). We must, therefore, not confuse decentralization and deconcentration which, as Lemieux, Brown and Morin argue, "consists specifically in transferring power and decision-making to an administrative authority, to subordinate agents that remain within the internal hierarchy" (Issalys and Lemieux 2002: 244).

The distinction between centralization/decentralization and deconcentration is essential to understanding why the Canadian federal system cannot, despite what many scholars suggest, be considered to be totally decentralized (Courchene 1995; Macdougall 1991; Dion 1992; Dion 1994; Leslie 1993; Tully 1995b; Valaskakis and Fournier 1995). There are also political actors actively involved in the politics of decentralization who confuse this dynamic with deconcentration. A more accurate conclusion would be to say that Canada has adopted an approach that favours a certain, albeit limited, form of deconcentration, while preserving its centrist tradition. We will explain why Canada has adopted this approach in the following section.

The process of centralization can take many forms and many routes. The constitutional route is the least traveled. Judicial interpretation of powers can supplement amendments that have been adopted by slightly or significantly, depending upon the circumstances, modifying the interpretation of powers devolved to one or another order of government. For many, the entrenchment of the 1982 Canadian Charter of Rights and Freedoms reinforced this process by profoundly changing, and in a lasting manner, the symbolic representation of the Canadian political environment and by imposing constraints that reinforced the legitimacy of the central government. In Canadian political history, another powerful centralizing instrument has greatly contributed to the expansion of the federal government's capacity to influence the priorities of the federal units: the use of the federal spending power. Finally, at the administrative level, the centralizing dynamic has become manifest through the more or less constraining consensus that binds governments to 'national' objectives that are principally defined by the federal government.

The constitutional voice or the voices of the Constitution

As Andrée Lajoie argues, three types of constitutional instruments are responsible for the centralization of the Canadian federation. In the first place, "the constitution itself, which sets out the division of powers and, simultaneously, the theories of judicial interpretation that will be applied to it and to the constitutional practices of the executive" (Lajoie 2005: 2). It becomes clear that the "constitutive" power subordinates the federated communities, which are left to the mercy of the federal judges' interpretation of the Constitution. Therefore, a certain form of centralization arises from judicial decisions enabled by the constitutional division of power as well as by governmental practices developed at the margins (Ibid.). In this respect, the Canadian federal state could be seen as a decentralized unitary state because, under the terms of the Constitution, the federated entities are subordinated to the state (Frankel 1986: 92). Furthermore:

> [...] it is not so much the original text of the Canadian Constitution that is responsible for the current centralization of legislative powers or the centralization of the executive powers related to them. Rather, this centralization is the result of judicial interpretations of the division of powers and from government practices that have developed at its margins (Lajoie 2008: 144).

The Privy Council has, in effect, granted new instruments of centralization to the Supreme Court of Canada, which has taken advantage of them to define an increasingly unilateral, dialogical and standardized federalism (Lajoie 2005: 3). The problem arises equally from the fact that the Supreme Court "has not defined a federal theory that would have allowed it to resolve contentious issues involving the division of powers through recourse to an overarching vision of the Canadian federation and its evolution" (Brouillet 2004: 63). Consequently, by relying excessively upon the principle of exclusivity and by applying this de-compartmentalized vision only when doing so facilitated the exercise of federal powers, the Supreme Court has abandoned the core federal principle of the Canadian constitutional order (Ibid., 62). As Benoît Pelletier, former Quebec Minister of Canadian Intergovernmental Affairs states, judicial decisions can produce effects that structure the constitutional order in important ways, such that "today, we see developing a centralizing trend in federal legislation that cannot but threaten federalism itself" (B. Pelletier 2004).[7] The laws that have been thus adopted, which are based on an essentially functional understanding of federalism, have unfortunately sometimes been reinforced by decisions of the Supreme Court of Canada.

Beyond judicial interpretation and the role of the Supreme Court, Réjean Pelletier claims that the general interventionist powers articulated in the preamble of Section 91 regarding the residual power, the declaratory power, and in practice the federal spending power, as well as the instruments of control entrusted to central authorities (the powers of disallowance, reservation and nomination) have altered the fine balance of the division of powers. In so doing, they contribute to greater centralization. This centralization comes about, according to Pelletier, on account of a never corrected "deficiency" in the Canadian federation (R. Pelletier 2008: 227). Lawrence Anderson contests this notion: "While the British North America Act did have a strong centralizing tendency built to it, the provinces were able to resist some of its centralizing features through their control over local issues, like direct taxation, property, civil rights municipal institutions and education" (Anderson 2007: 197). Certainly, the diversity of regional cultures and interests was preserved. However, considering the economic powers and the important general powers that were granted to the central government, the Canadian federation tended more towards centralization than decentralization (R. Pelletier 2008: 53).

Along the same lines, we can also attribute a centralizing effect to the Canadian Charter of Rights and Freedoms of 1982. As Eugénie Brouillet explains, the entrenchment of the Charter ignored national pluralism in the Canadian state. Originally, the spirit and letter of the federal regime took into account the national aspirations of the Quebec nation. The *British North America Act* of 1867 was based on a compromise between two cultures and was intended to establish a genuine federation that would be capable of accommodating the Quebecois cultural identity. In fact, Brouillet adds, it is the identity concerns of the Quebec nation that justify the adoption of a federal regime in Canada. Quebec agreed to the federal compromise in the first place because it was supposed to take its concerns into account and recognize its character (Brouillet 2005). The Charter was imposed at a pan-Canadian level without taking into consideration this state of affairs, namely that the federation rests first and foremost on differentiated conventions and cultures. James Tully eloquently summarizes one of the centralizing effects following the adoption of the Charter:

> When the Quebec Assembly seek to preserve and enhance Quebec's character as a modern, predominantly French-speaking society, it finds that its traditional sovereignty in this area is capped by a Charter in terms of which all its legislation must be phrased and justified, but from which any recognition of Quebec's distinct character has been completely excluded. The effect of the Charter is thus to assimilate Quebec to a pan-Canadian national culture, exactly what the 1867 constitution, according to Lord Watson, was established to prevent. Hence, from this perspective, the Charter is "imperial" in the precise sense of the term that has always been used to justify independence (Tully 2009: 163).

In the same vein, R. Knopff and F. L. Morton argue that the Charter opened the door to a government of judges and that "important policy determinations that were previously the prerogative of legislatures will now be made by the Supreme [C]ourt sitting at the apex of a single judicial hierarchy" (Knopff and Morton 1985: 147). Given that some aspects of public policy are developed by federal entities, the Charter has contributed to undermining the balance in the division of powers between the federal and provincial governments (Cardinal 2000: 47). The centralizing character of the Charter was underlined by its inclusion of constitutional obligations in regards to bilingualism and multiculturalism, which greatly increased the symbolic status of these elements to the point that they are today considered to be fundamental aspects of Canadian nationality (Knopff and Morton 1985: 161). In sum, the first centralizing effect of the Charter was to considerably enlarge the field of constitutional control over government action, which, until then, had been primarily concerned with ensuring that the division of legislative powers was respected (Issalys and Lemieux 2002: 23).

James B. Kelly and Janet L. Hiebert nevertheless call into question the centralizing effect that we attribute to the Charter. They believe that the move to determine the constitutionality of laws on the basis of Charter principles has not produced the centralizing effect that we attribute to it. More concretely, they argue that the rulings of the Supreme Court reveal a certain receptivity towards federalism, and that the Charter does not thwart the principle of autonomy. In its rulings involving the Charter, the Court has adopted an approach that reconciles fundamental rights with federalism (J. B. Kelly 2001: 322, 354; Hiebert 1999).[8] For his part, José Woehrling would claim that the centralizing effects of determining constitutionality on the basis of the Canadian Charter of Rights and Freedoms derive from the transfer of decision-making power on social, economic and political questions from representative provincial bodies to federal judicial bodies (Woehrling 2009). Furthermore, in the long run, the Court, whose members are appointed by the federal government without any provincial input, favours an increase in the political legitimacy of the central government's powers on account of the organic and institutional ties that bind members of the Supreme Court and federal politicians (Ibid., 265). Guy Laforest continues in the same vein: "The 1982 Charter deterritorialises conflicts, removes them from their provincial realms in order to place them in a pan-Canadian politico-judicial arena in which they are adjudicated by a Supreme Court that is an arm of the central state" (Laforest 1992: 132).

Finally, another centralizing impact of the Charter is that of granting the power to order any measure ('remedy') judged appropriate to the same courts that have the power to define constitutionality by determining what constitutes an infringement of the rights and freedoms protected by the Charter (Issalys and Lemieux 2002: 23). In this sense, section 24 of the Charter creates a right to reparation that is distinct from that which can be obtained through civil law (Ibid.).[9] Consequently, many interest and pressure groups that establish ties with the federal authorities who finance them have recourse to the Charter. In this sense, it is clear for Woehrling that "[c]onstitutional protection for individual rights restricts a group's collective freedom to govern itself" (Woehrling 2009: 274).

What is more, the regime instituted by the Canadian Charter of Rights and Freedoms, in keeping with the *Official Languages Act*,[10] essentially presents a symmetric and falsely egalitarian vision of relations between anglophones and francophones in Canada. On the whole, this regime equates the situation of the majority francophone population in Quebec with that of the majority anglophone population in the rest of Canada, and that of the anglophone minority in Quebec with that of the francophone minorities in the other provinces and territories. It does not take into consideration that, even if francophones comprise the majority in Quebec, they remain a minority in Canada and, *a fortiori*, in America. Political philosopher Will Kymlicka gives an accurate account of the situation when he affirms that "the intended outcomes of these policies is clear: to centralize all political and legal power in forums dominated by the majority group; to privilege that group's language and culture in all public institutions, which are then diffused throughout the territory of the state; and to make minority languages and cultures invisible in public space" (Kymlicka 2007: 62–63).

The federal spending power: when Ottawa plays generous

Besides the interpretation of jurisprudence and of the initial division of powers, the centralist thesis applies also to the argument that the central government claims for itself the right to spend in areas of provincial jurisdiction, and to do so with money it collects through taxation (Quebec 1956, vol. 1: 203, 223). Henri Brun and Guy Tremblay describe the federal spending power as the power of a government to "spend money in matters that fall under the jurisdiction of the other order of government without legislating, regulating or directing them" (Brun and Tremblay 2002: 431). Still, the exercise of this power exerts constant and direct pressure on the federal balance. As stated more than fifty years ago by the Royal Commission of Inquiry on Constitutional Problems:

> By allowing the central government access to the main sources of revenue and by admitting the principle of subsidies from the very beginning, even though it was makeshift, it made of the former a millionaire who would soon accustom himself to play the part of the generous donor, while it made of the provinces perpetual beggars which, most of the time, were only too glad to accept offers of help from the Dominion (Quebec 1956, vol. 2: 212).

In this sense, the federal state no longer needs the powers of reservation and disallowance, nor the declaratory power in order for it to interfere in areas of jurisdiction that were not granted to it. It has only to use its spending power (R. Pelletier 2008: 37). The frequent use of this power allows the federal government to justify maintaining the current fiscal structure and perpetuates a certain imbalance between the legislative capacities of the two orders of government, what has come to be known as the fiscal imbalance. Therefore, the federal spending power and the fiscal imbalance mutually reinforce one another.

In other words, the current division of fiscal resources between the two orders of government allows the federal state, in light of its responsibilities, to spend significant sums of money, exacerbating its tendency to interfere—often by unilateral initiatives for which funds are directly transferred to individuals or to organizations—in areas that fall outside its constitutional powers (B. Pelletier 2004). Furthermore, this fiscal advantage leads the federal government to attach conditions to its financial transfers that limit the powers of the provinces and that do not always respect their needs, their priorities or their particularities. These conditions often amount to regulation of the area of jurisdiction in which the funds are spent, even though constitutional law recognizes them as a provincial areas of jurisdiction. These considerations lead Réjean Pelletier, for example, to assert that it is important for each order of government to have access to fiscal resources in order to fully assume its responsibilities without finding itself in a situation of political subordination. As Maurice Croisat also underlined, "within the conception of dualism, federal finances must allow each level of government access to sufficient revenues to finance their expenses, given that financial autonomy is a necessary condition for the exercise of political autonomy" (Croisat 1995: 83). More than fifty years ago, this was also one of the arguments of the Tremblay Commission:

> Quebec, however, has always preferred to base the security of its existence on the freedom of its government and, since freedom is impossible without having the command of stable financial and fiscal sources, it knows only too well that the fate of its autonomy and that of its free development hinges, and will continue in the future to hinge, even more closely on this point (Quebec 1956, vol. 1: 185).

From the federal spending power—which allows the federal government to intervene in areas of provincial jurisdiction—to the lack of fiscal resources, we can add the attitude of the Supreme Court which is of the opinion that a conditional transfer in an area of provincial jurisdiction is not a legislative action. However, a conditional transfer that imposes national standards can clearly be an attempt on the part of federal officials to do indirectly what they cannot do directly, namely, legislate in areas of provincial jurisdiction (Brouillet 2004: 32).

In this context, it is not surprising that the federal spending power is perceived as a powerful instrument of centralization. We do not aim to contest the relevance of these interventions or the adequacy of these policies for meeting the presumed needs of the citizens, nor do we seek to question the support they can give to federal government policies. It is nevertheless important to underline that use of this instrument of public policy has contributed to consolidating the capacity of one order of government to intervene in the other's areas of jurisdiction. It is also important to remember that this power has never been officially recognized or confirmed by the Supreme Court of Canada; it rests, therefore, on fragile constitutional grounds that, for obvious reasons, no political actor would seek to have confirmed.[11] As we have seen, this practice is far from being consequence-free. On the contrary, it constitutes an attack on the federal principle. For Marc-Antoine Adam:

> The unlimited spending power thesis does not work. It has no basis in the constitution and is at odds with many of our constitutional rules and principles. Nor has it been endorsed by the Privy Council or the Supreme Court of Canada. The unlimited spending power thesis is best described as an ex post construct designed to provide a legal explanation for Ottawa's involvement in areas of provincial jurisdiction, particularly in the social field in the aftermath of the Great Depression. As it is currently articulated, it is incompatible with constitutional federalism, a crucially important concept in Canada, if only from Quebec's perspective, because it protects minority rights. This may well explain why the Supreme Court has never formally accepted the unlimited spending power thesis (Adam 2008: 223).

To this day, the central government views its spending power as an instrument that is in no way limited by the division of powers (Lajoie 2008).[12] The decision rendered in December 2008 on the legality of accumulating employment insurance surpluses strongly confirms this view. In this decision, the Court again refused to rule on the constitutionality of the spending power.[13]

In spite of these constitutional ambiguities, or perhaps because of them, the federal government has, on more than one occasion, expressed a desire to circumscribe the 'supposed' federal spending power so as to limit its applicability rather than contest its very existence in the courts. Both the Meech Lake Accord of 1987 and the Charlottetown Agreement of 1992, two failed attempts at constitutional amendment, contained clauses designed to circumscribe the federal spending power. Essentially, the wording of these clauses would have entrenched the right of opting-out in the Constitution by allowing any province that chose not to participate in a new Canada-wide federal shared-cost program in an area of exclusive provincial jurisdiction to receive fair compensation from the federal government so long as it implemented a program or a measure in keeping with the 'national objectives' of the corresponding federal program. Despite the failure of these constitutional amendments, the effort nevertheless continued with the proposal put forward by Prime Minister Jean Chrétien's Liberal government to include the issue of the federal spending power in the Social Union Framework Agreement. Strenuously opposed by the Quebec government, this agreement has yet to produce any concrete results. The Quebec government saw in this proposal a means of intervening in key social sectors by delivering funds directly to individuals or organizations without the consent of the affected province. It also objected to a number of deficiencies and important ambiguities regarding the federal spending power that, as we are reminded, has no clear constitutional basis.

More recently, Prime Minister Stephen Harper's government reiterated the idea of constraining the federal spending power in its 2008 Speech from the Throne. In effect, "in the words of the Throne Speech, the Conservative government promised it would place formal limits on the use of the federal spending power for new shared-cost programs in areas of exclusive provincial jurisdiction" (Mendes 2008: 231). Presented in the media as the "Harper Doctrine" on the federal spending power, this was nevertheless disparaged by many who saw in it nothing more than an electoral strategy designed to appeal to the Quebec electorate (Ibid., 247).[14] For Eroll Mendes, who also criticizes it, "the major danger, however, with this political maneuvering is that the very attempt to build firewalls through the use of tax points might not only permanently hobble the spending power, but undermine one of the very foundations of federalism itself" (Ibid.). These elements correspond less with guiding federal principles than they do with political objectives that accord with the priorities of analysts and political actors. Standing in defence of the federal spending power, which supposedly derives from the constitutional powers of taxation (Section 91 (3)), public property (Section 91 (1A)) and use of consolidated funds (Section 106), Mendes, adopting a decidedly pan-Canadian or 'national' approach, phrases the necessity of his appeal to consolidate the Canadian social state in terms of universal values:

> At its core, the modern welfare state has the need to see that social inequalities do not reach a level where social stability is at risk. This is central to the rationales of both the establishment of the system of equalization payments as well as the rise of the federal spending power" (Ibid., 228).

The goal of Prime Minister Harper's Conservative government's maneuver was a return to a compartmentalized vision of federalism aimed at limiting transfers from rich provinces to those in the greatest need. Furthermore, those who support the federal spending power have, "claimed that decentralization results in the sacrifice of both efficiency and equity. Therefore, it can be inferred that the spending power promotes both efficiency and equity" (Ibid., 237–238). The instrumental rationality of federalism resurfaces here in the name of the principle of equity, obliterating the principles of autonomy and collaboration essential to any regime meant to be federal. Unilateralism finds itself a 'federal' justification, which according to us, appears to be nonsense.

In a more nuanced manner, Harvey Lazar acknowledges that competing understandings of the spending power reflect opposing concepts of the Canadian political community. He writes that "the spending power [...] is more than a mere instrument of public policy. The power is also a symbol. It acts as a signaling device about the kind of federation that the federal government desires for Canada" (Lazar 2008: 126). The provinces can accept transfers for practical and evident financial reasons. But there remains, more so than Lazar acknowledges, a logic according to which the ends of federalism are determined solely by the central government through a non-federal process. In reality, the federal government would require the participation of the provinces in collaboratively defining common priorities. At the end of the day, the centralizing dynamic is not contested but rather defended through arguments that further distance us from the principles that should govern relations in a federal regime.

At the same time, from the angle of public administration, the centralizing dynamic is presented as "an organizational process that gathers all of the powers in one central body that, directly or through intermediaries over which it exercises a hierarchical authority, is the only one to make administrative decisions" (Mercier 2004: 67). Centralization is sometimes accompanied by a deconcentration that allows agents, hierarchically-dependant on the central institutions, to have a certain power to take initiative while maintaining their double responsibility to respect directives emanating from the centre and to be accountable to it (Ibid.). This form of devolution differs from decentralization, which is "a process that consists in the transfer of roles, responsibilities, and powers from the central administration to an autonomous and distinct administration" (Ibid., 68). As Jean Mercier states:

> ...a truly de-centralized body makes decisions relatively
> independently of the central administration [...] there is
> territorial de-centralization when the state allows a body
> that represents a collectivity to have limited jurisdic-
> tion over a given territory and a form of autonomy with
> respect to certain responsibilities (Ibid.).

Additional requirements for achieving a real degree of
decentralization are sectoral autonomy (administrative control over particular areas); political autonomy (the decentralized entity is headed by elected representatives who
exercise power without being subordinate); and financial
autonomy (power to establish its own budget and to assure
that it is properly financed).

The distinction between decentralization and deconcentration is, unfortunately, often unclear in many writings on
federalism. This ambiguity can be explained, in part, by the
fact that:

> Two broad systems offer opposing solutions to the issues
> of territorial administration that arise in Western democ-
> racies. The first, founded on the British tradition of self-
> government, has for a long time entailed the existence of
> decentralized territorial collectivities. The second, attrib-
> uted to the Jacobin and Napoleonic ideology, gave rise
> to the theory of deconcentration and was put into place
> through the French prefectorial system (Ibid., 70).

Various authors state, therefore, that Canadian federalism
is, territorially and sectorally, highly decentralized (Bernard
1996). Others, such as James Iain Gow and Bruno Théret,
are more critical and argue instead that political decentralization between the federal and provincial governments is
different from administrative decentralization between the
provinces and municipalities. The reason being that "political decentralization that is based on a constitutional text or
agreement cannot, in principle, be unilaterally modified
by one of the parties, whereas in the case of administrative
decentralization, the central administration (here the pro-

vincial governments) sets the legislative agenda and has a greater right of oversight and control" (Gow 1992: 85, 88). In sum, it would be more accurate to speak of a decentralized unitary state (Théret uses the term 'empire') rather than of a federation (Théret 2005: 100).

On the so-called decentralized character of Canadian federalism

The arguments that we have presented are not, in themselves, new. However, they remain prevalent and their refutation does not always succeed in persuading people of the contrary position. In addition, the proponents of the decentralization thesis, much as they strive to find other criteria, often cannot discount these facts, and their counter arguments fail.

To summarize, two sets of arguments have been advanced to suggest that Canada is heavily decentralized. The first rests on the increased political capacity of the provinces, the second on a set of 'indicators' that, taken in turn, are not entirely persuasive.

A first approach to addressing the question rests on the increased political capacities of the provincial governments. The argument rests on a zero-sum game: if the provinces are more 'powerful', the federal government must have 'lost' some of its powers. The views of Donald Smiley are especially representative of this approach. His argument rests on the assertion that the process of:

> ...[m]odernization has not led to centralization in the Canadian federal system but rather to the power, assertiveness, and competence of the provinces. Furthermore, the provinces where modernization has proceeded most rapidly are those most insistent about preserving and extending their autonomy (Smiley 1984: 59).

Therefore, the affirmation of provincial powers would have put a brake on the centralization of powers in the hands of the central government. Garth Stevenson sees in the growth of provincial bureaucracies since World War

II an indicator that the federated entities have gained in importance, power, and authority (Stevenson 2004: 73). Along exactly the same lines, Alan Cairns has already suggested that:

> ...[c]ontrary to virtually all predictions, post-World Canadian politics has not displayed an irreversible trend to centralization (...) instead the provinces, aided by secular trends which have enhanced the practical significance of their constitutionally-based legislative authority, and by deliberate improvement of their own bureaucratic power and capacity, have given a new salience to the politics of federalism and territory-based diversities it encompasses, reflects and fosters (Cairns 1977: 720).

All in all, the argument amounts to reiterating the claim that the development of the welfare state came about through an increased activism amongst provincial governments. The provinces, therefore, succeeded in counter-balancing the centralizing tendencies that had marked the previous periods. Canadian federalism thus defined itself by the implementation of collaborative mechanisms that contributed greatly to re-shaping intergovernmental relations to the benefit of the federated entities that showed themselves to be concerned with preserving their autonomy, increasing their room to maneuver financially, engaging in hard-fought negotiations with the central government to acquire the means that would allow them to implement new programs aimed at responding to the new needs as identified by the population in matters of education, social protection, health and economic development. The provinces even became more active in international relations, notably to attract foreign investments, but also, in the case of Quebec, for reasons of identity (Paquin 2005). All in all, these observations emphasize the absence of a centralizing trend. In its absence, the provinces were able to advance their own priorities, thereby obliging the federal government to negotiate with them and to share the authority that it had previously held alone.

Other authors have instead sought to demonstrate the greatly decentralized character of the Canadian federation. Among them, the most notable is certainly former university professor, former President of the Privy Council, and former Canadian Minister of Intergovernmental Affairs (and briefly leader of the Liberal Party of Canada) the Hon. Stéphane Dion. On the basis of indicators such as the extent of fiscal decentralization, the division of powers, and federal transfers as a percentage of the total fiscal revenue of the provinces, he argues that the decentralized character of our federation is plainly evident when Canada is compared with other federations. We would certainly love to share his enthusiasm. But his proof, which should be persuasive, is not always so. For example, Dion argues:

> ...the analysis of data from 1959 to the beginning of the 1990s demonstrates that Ottawa and Berne are the two federal governments which control the smallest portion of public revenues and expenditures. The Canadian provinces are far more powerful then the Swiss cantons in this regard (Dion 1996: 107).

While this is an interesting fact, the measure that he proposes does not take into account municipalities. Comparisons with other federations cannot be limited "to the autonomous revenues and the public expenditures of central and regional governments, but must include those of municipal governments" (Ibid., 106–107). The reason for this is that the central government's contribution must be compared with the combined total of regional and other municipal governments because "the fiscal decentralization of a region or a province towards its municipalities would have the same effect otherwise, in an international comparison, as the fiscal centralization of a province or a province toward the central government" (Ibid.). Once these elements are taken into consideration, the Canadian federation becomes perhaps not so decentralized after all (Ibid.). As Jennifer Wallner explains, authors who undertake this type of analysis:

...need to build municipalities into the equation in the evaluation effect of decentralization [...] the lack of constitutional status for municipal governments and their off-pro-
claimed characterization as 'creature of the provinces' has
allowed researchers to overlook the further decentralization that comes with local government (Wallner 2008: 174).

Let us consider this other idea that decentralization is
associated with an increase in the influence of provincial
governments at the expense of the federal government. In
order for there to be genuine decentralization, the federal
government would have to relinquish its authority over
federal jurisdictions. If the federal government continues to participate in the establishment of mechanisms to
which the provinces are subordinate that constrain policy
making, evaluation, planning or control—as is the present case—then we are faced less with decentralization than
what we defined earlier as deconcentration (Rouillard and
Rocher 1996). According to Rocher and Rouillard, even if
new mechanisms were developed that, ideally, would break
with the unilateral approach that characterizes contemporary federalism, decentralization would continue along a
path marked by multilateral accords aimed at defining standardized norms and objectives that the provinces would
have to respect (Rocher and Rouillard 1998). To those who
see in this a gain for the provinces and a convincing form of
decentralization, we offer two answers. Firstly, it is wrong
to conclude that there is decentralization:

...when provinces or regions run budget deficits, the government increases its total revenues through internal or
external loans and, consequently, reduces the proportion
of conditional federal transfers as a percentage of total
revenues without there being a decentralization of the
federation (Rouillard and Rocher 1996: 109).

We must bear in mind the fact that genuine decentralization should include a transfer to the provinces of authority
over jurisdictions that was originally assigned to the federal

government. If the federal government maintains common managerial powers or practices a form of 'micro-management' in an attempt to be more efficient, we must, as André Burelle argued, admit that it leads us away from decentralization and, what is more, away from federalism itself. Despite the fact that the provinces are well positioned to administer their power to manage the system (Rocher and Rouillard 1998: 240), the decentralization that is in question here comes closer to the principle of subsidiarity, in that the latter emphasizes principles of efficiency in an attempt to re-think the role and size of the state.

Regarding fiscal resources and transfer payments, we must not forget that even if the provinces are more independent and rely less and less on federal transfers, the fiscal imbalance remains a reality and is likely to grow because of the fact that the costs of programs that fall under provincial areas of jurisdiction are likely to grow more quickly than do those of programs administered by the federal government. In fact, it is becoming more and more difficult for certain provinces that lack a sufficient tax base to finance health, education, social services and even municipal affairs. This situation leaves them more financially vulnerable. A number of provinces have been reduced to dependency on Ottawa for funds that are delivered through transfer payments and other programs. This aid is often attended with certain conditions that contribute, for the provinces, to a progressive subjection to federal wishes and priorities and, consequently, to a loss of autonomy. Even if these transfers do contribute to diminishing the horizontal fiscal (or financial) imbalance, that is to say, the differences in per capita spending amongst the provinces, they have little effect on the vertical fiscal imbalance, which is to say the advantage that the federal government enjoys over the provinces as a result of appropriating for itself a disproportionate share of the tax base. This latter form of imbalance is more serious than the first because it has a greater effect on federal relations. In addition, "we can easily imagine a situation in which the central government reduces the amount of its conditional transfers without reducing the number or scope of the national standards to which provincial or regional governments must adhere. Federal transfer drops, but federal control remains unchanged" (Rouillard and Rocher 1996: 108).

A good example is Prime Minister Stephen Harper's 2007 Budget that was supposed to modify the equalization formula to render it more 'equitable'. The federal government announced in the budget that it was implementing the reform measures recommended in the O'Brien report, the key element in his solution to the fiscal imbalance in Canada. The Quebec government subsequently indicated in its budget of May 24, 2007 that this decision would 'largely' respond to its demands. Nevertheless, on November 3, 2008, the Government of Canada announced its intention to unilaterally modify the equalization program. It was the first time in the history of this program that the federal government did not consult with the provinces before making significant changes to the formula. The federal government's objective was to implement three new 'ceilings', thereby depriving the beneficiary provinces of important funds.[15]

In sum, to consider the Canadian federation as highly decentralized is to conveniently forget about the multiple constraints imposed (often, it is true, by means of negotiation) by the central government. It is also to ignore the fact that the growth of provincial interventionism has been accompanied by a larger presence of the federal government in areas of provincial jurisdiction, which has rendered more and more opaque, if not nearly obsolete, the original letter and spirit of the Canadian Constitution. Depending on our political orientations and preferences, we can either lament or rejoice in this development. But neither supports the argument that presents the Canadian federation as highly decentralized.

Conclusion: to re-federalize Canada?

Debates about the supposed decentralized character of the Canadian federation mask another debate that we take to be even more fundamental. As we underlined at the beginning of this chapter, no discussion of federalism can avoid an exploration of the normative principles that should animate every federal state. The notions of autonomy, of non-subordination, of participation and of solidarity all point to the requirement that the political regime reflect the constitutive principle of equality. As Delpéré and Verdussen remind us:

> ...unlike decentralization, federalism is incompatible with a power structure that results in subordination [...] 'There can be no sovereign in a federal state,' wrote Carl Friedrich. Or more precisely, only the Constitution— which establishes the relationships between the federal state and federated communities—is sovereign in this type of state structure (Delpéré and Verdussen 2005: 197).

Thus, analyses of the centralization/decentralization dynamic rest on different premises regarding the definition of the Canadian political community. For the many who believe that equality amongst citizens requires identical treatment throughout the country and that provincial governments must subscribe to norms, standards and conditions that assure an equality of treatment through access to relatively identical public policies, the fact that the central government occupies the centre of the political chessboard is unproblematic. From this perspective, 'excessive' decentralization is viewed negatively because it leads to a diversity of policies that reflect the preferences of citizens who are territorially confined to their provincial space. Hardly a caricature, 'federal' citizenship is equated with 'national' citizenship in which the central government is seen as the protector of a certain uniformity of treatment. This is what Keith Banting pointed out in regards to the way in which fiscal arrangements are finalized. We believe that this perspective can apply equally to the general understanding that has formed as to the role assigned to the two orders of government:

[O]ur fiscal arrangements reflect choices about the nature of political community: one vision which celebrates Canada as a community embracing all citizens from one side of the country to the other, and the second which celebrates Canada as an interlinked set of regional communities or a community of communities. Seen in this light, our fiscal arrangements represent one of the ways in which we define the social programs to which we are committed, the nature of democracy that we are going to practice, and the conception of community we are going to reinforce. The issues may be technical, and in some immediate sense the debates are inevitably about money and power. But our fiscal arrangements embody big choices about the kind of country we want to be (Banting 205: 37–38).

Another perspective, particularly well established in Quebec, but evident elsewhere in Canada as well, stresses the fact that the federal regime is based on founding communities that joined together originally without wanting to amalgamate or to acquire a supranational citizenship. As Burelle reminds us, the political communities simply decided to confer upon the central government the powers that would be best exercised at the level of the union, while the provinces would preserve their full sovereignty in local affairs, in keeping with the principle of subsidiarity. In this context, the functionalist approach to federalism, articulated in terms of the reinforcement of the undifferentiated Canadian political community, is rather allergic to any form of 'decentralization' that would favour the heterogeneity of communities (Burelle 2005: 449).

Of course, a close analysis of the policies that are considered favourable to centralization could demonstrate that the critiques of them are too severe or lacking in nuance. For example, the conditions attached to federal transfers are judged by some to be far less constraining than are those found in other federations (Watts 1999b). Furthermore, as G. Boychuk demonstrates, there is appreciable diversity in the means through which the welfare state has been established in Canada (Boychuk 1998). Therefore, the provinces would have been able to successfully resist the encroachments of the federal government into their exclusive areas of jurisdiction. This nuanced reading would not, however, allow us to forget that the development of the central government's interventionism nevertheless manifested itself in a considerable increase of its influence in the policy sectors that, under the terms of the Constitution, fall under provincial jurisdiction. That the provinces opposed these encroachments seems to us clear, as does the fact that these encroachments have been numerous and constant.

The principal problem, however, arises from a flawed understanding of the functioning of the federal state and of the concomitant division of powers. This produces a weak adherence to principles that feed, what we have designated as, a federal culture.[16] In fact, the first phenomenon reinforces the second. The weakness of the federal culture in Canada does nothing but accentuate the 're-deployment' of an approach considered to be 'national' that is, furthermore, desired by the population.

After the failure of the Meech Lake Accord, while directing the Federal-Provincial Relations Office in Montreal, André Burelle proposed a 'therapy' designed to support the recognition of the right to difference that would be accompanied by a decentralization of powers and fiscal resources. In return, the provinces would have agreed to participate more actively in defining common objectives and minimal common standards in order to reinforce the economic and social union in Canada (Burelle 1995). The path that Burelle proposed, although interesting insofar as it would allow a 're-federalization' of Canada, is not practical in a context in which the political forces, supported by the overwhelming majority of Canadian intellectuals and academics, continue to deny the fact that Canadian federalism is heavily centralized. In other words, the denial of a centralized dynamic, or worse, the mantra claiming that Canadian federalism is one of the most decentralized in the world, cannot open the door to a discussion on the necessity of decentralization.

In fact, at the risk of appearing to be iconoclasts, we believe that the idea that federalism enshrines mutually shared and agreed upon normative principles is dead. We are left with nothing but the 'federal' politico-administrative apparatus, the power relations it gives rise to, piecemeal arrangements, and the inevitable ideological (and partisan) conflicts that will ensure that much more ink will be spilled over the debate on centralization/decentralization (in order to arrive at more or less the same conclusions) over the coming decades.

Endnotes

[1] "...federalism has increasingly been presented as an institutional panacea in states characterized by the plurality of identities. The rationale behind this claim is obvious: federalism is a pluralist political solution that aims to reconcile divergent but overlapping identites; so it may offer hope for societies characterized by such pluralism."

[2] André Burelle adds that "for George-Etienne Cartier and for the other leaders of French Canada, this only confirmed a right acquired in the *1774 Quebec Act*. In order to divert them from the American revolution, the British Parliament had granted to French Canadians living in Quebec, the right to preserve their language, their religion, their civil law, their Seigneurial regime, in other words their French way of life through which they would form a 'distinct society' in North America" [our translation].

[3] See also: Comité spécial du Parti libéral du Québec sur l'avenir politique et constitutionnel de la société québécoise, Benoît Pelletier, (ed.), *Un Projet pour le Québec. Affirmation, autonomie, leadership*, Montréal, Parti libéral du Québec, 2001: "Provincial autonomy in their areas of jurisdiction constitutes one of the key principles of federalism. Thus, in order for genuine federalism to exist and to subsist, the provinces cannot be subordinated to the federal level of government. Any federal practice that would subjugate the provinces to the federal government or tip the balance of federal-provincial relations represents a deviation from the federal formula." p. 46 [our translation].

[4] Furthermore, according to Brouillet: "In two very important judicial references—re: Resolution to amend the Constitution, [1981] 1 S.C.R. 753 and the Reference re Secession of Quebec, [1998] 2 S.C.R. 217—the Supreme Court explicitly invoked the federal principal in answering

the legal questions that were brought before it. These two decisions constitute by far the longest discussions of federalism ever conducted by the Supreme Court. The Court also made reference to federalism in certain decision concerning intergovernmental relations and the federal spending power" [our translation].

5 As Marc Chevrier has stated: "the notion of balance is particularly present in the writings of legal scholars and political scientists in Québec. It is the criterion according to which Henri Brun and Guy Tremblay assess the constitutional division of powers and the division of resources in Canada. They argue that the balance of powers between governments in a federal regime is not a panacea, but it can serve to ensure the long term preservation of the very essence of the federal regime, namely the respective autonomy of the two levels of government."

6 Besides the authors mentioned, we must also acknowledge the invaluable contributions of the following: Alain-G. Gagnon, Daniel Jacques, Guy Laforest, Michael Ignatieff, John Ralston Saul, Daniel Weinstock, and more recently, Eugénie Brouillet Jocelyn Maclure, and Xavier Gélinas.

7 In two cases in which the debate dealt with the theory of national dimensions (originally called "national concerns"), the Supreme Court endorsed the federal legislative measures on the basis of the theory. RJR-MacDonald Inc. c. Canada (Procureur général), [1995] 3 R.C.S. 199 et R. c. Hydro-Québec, [1997] 3 R.C.S. 213.

8 "In essence, the centralization thesis is not an accurate characterization of the relationship between Charter review and federal diversity, as the number of cases where the Court has nullified provincial status are few and far between, and, more importantly, the nullifications have not taken place in core areas of provincial responsibilities" (J. B. Kelly June 2001: 322, 354).

9 Section 24 states that: "Anyone whose rights or freedoms, as guaranteed by this Charter, have been infringed or denied may apply to a court of competent jurisdiction to obtain such remedy as the court considers appropriate and just in the circumstances."

10 Loi sur les langues officielles, S.R.C. 1970, c. O-2. This federal statute was adopted by the Parliament in 1969. It declares that French and English enjoy an equal status, equal rights and privileges as to their usage in all of the institutions of Parliament and of the Government of Canada. In 1988, a new Official Languages Act was passed into law.

11 Over the past two decades, the Supreme Court has refered to the federal spending power in five cases: YMHA Jewish Community Centre of Winnipeg Inc. v Brown, [1989] 1 R.C.S. 1532; Renvoi relatif au Régime d'assistance publique du Canada (C.-B.), [1991] 2 R.C.S. 525; Finlay v

Canada (Ministre des Finances), [1993] 1 R.C.S. 108; Chaoulli v Québec (Procureur général), [2005] 1 R.C.S. 791.0.; Eldridge v Colombie-Britannique (Procureur général), [1997] 3 R.C.S. 624.

[12] Andrée Lajoie, *supra* note 47, "Current Exercises of The Federal spending power: What does the Constitutions Say About It?": "The federal spending power, which imposes conditions that are equivalent to the exercise of normative power in fields of provincial jurisdiction, is still not part of this Constitution, unless more weight is given to a decision of the Court of Appeal of Alberta than to all of the precedents of the Privy Council and of the Supreme Court. In light of the direction and scope of all these decisions, it still seems accurate to say that the law is not yet decided on the matter of the constitutionality of the federal spending power in areas falling under provincial legislative jurisdiction".

[13] Le Syndicat national des employés de l'aluminium d'Arvida inc., et al, v Attorney General of Canada. Remember that the intervention of the Attorney-General of Quebec in this case was essentially defensive and was aimed at preventing the judicial recognition of a federal power that would not be limited by the division of powers. The Attorney-General, therefore, set about to defend Quebec's traditional position on the federal spending power, namely that it must be limited by the division of powers. On December 11, 2008, the Supreme Court of Canada handed down its unanimous decision in this case, written by Justice Lebel. In regards to the employment measures that had been recognised by the Quebec Court of Appeal as valid under the federal spending power, the Supreme Court ruled that their validity rested instead on the federal jurisdiction over employment insurance (article 91 (2A) of the *Constitution Act 1867*). The Court ruled that it was unnecessary to invoke the federal spending power in this case and did not rule on the scope of this power. The Court's silence on the question of the federal spending power and its decision to overturn the ruling of the Québec Court of Appeal on this point allows us to affirm that the question of the scope of this power has yet to be resolved.

[14] For Mendes, "Harper's rhetoric about the "outrageous spending power" may be only symbolic sound and fury, signifying not very much other than an attempt to lure Quebec voters. [...] The danger behind the possible legislative additions to the 1999 Social Union Framework Agreement implicit in the Harper government's stated desire to legislate restraints on the federal spending power is that if they are realized and not repealed, such changes could hobble the spending power itself by making it impractical and unrealistic in both economic and political terms to create any new national shared-cost programs, such as child care or pharmacare. These restrictions on new shared-cost programs would in effect put a firewall around the spending power, which may well have

been the objective of both Prime Minister Harper and his Quebec government allies. If this is the ultimate goal of the Harper Doctrine, it may be undone by the fact that it can only be achieved by federal legislation. While such legislation may be enacted by the current government, it could be repealed by any subsequent government which did not agree that destroying the ability of the federal government to promote vital national objectives in social development was conducive to meeting the real challenges of a competitive global economy".

[15] It also introduced an inequitable handling of Hydro-Québec's benefits linked to transport and the distribution of electricity. The press release of Québec's Minister of Finance denouncing this measure is available on the website of the Québec Ministry of Finance at the following address: www.finances.gouv.qc.ca.

[16] For more details, see Rocher 2009b and Fafard et al. 2010.

References

Adam, Marc-Antoine 2008 (Spring). "The Spending Power, Co-operative Federalism and Section 94." *Queen's Law Journal*, 34: 1: 175–224.

Anderson, Lawrence 2007. "Institutional Influences and Nationalism in Québec." *Nationalism and Ethnic Politics*, 13: 187–211.

Banting, Keith 2005. "Community, Federalism and Fiscal Arrangements in Canada." In *Canadian Fiscal Arrangements: What Works, What Might Work Better*, ed. Harvey Lazar. Montreal and Kingston, ON: McGill-Queen's University Press, 37–50.

Bernard, André 1996. *La vie politique au Québec et au Canada*. Quebec City: Ste-Foy Presses de l'Université du Québec.

Boychuk, Gerard 1998. *Patchworks of Purpose: The Development of Provincial Social Assistance Regimes in Canada*. Montreal: McGill-Queen's University Press.

Brouillet, Eugénie 2004. "La dilution du principe fédératif et la jurisprudence de la Cour suprême." *Les Cahiers de droit*, 45: 1: 7–67.

Brouillet, Eugénie 2005. *La négation de la nation. L'identité culturelle québécoise et le fédéralisme canadien*, coll. Cahiers des Amériques. Quebec: Septentrion.

Brun, Henri and Guy Tremblay 2002. *Droit constitutionnel*, 4th edition. Cowansville, Quebec: Éditions Yvon Blais.

Burelle, André 1995. *Le mal canadien, essai de diagnostic et esquisse d'une thérapie*. Montreal: Fides.

Burelle, André 2005. *Pierre Elliott Trudeau. L'intellectuel et le politique*. Montreal: Fides.

Burgess, Michael 2006. *Comparative Federalism: Theory and Practice*. London: Routledge.

Cairns, Alan C. 1977. "The Government and societies of Canadian Federalism." *Canadian Journal of Political Science*, 10: 4: 695–726.

Canada 1970. Supreme Court of Canada. *Loi sur les langues officielles*, S.R.C., c. O-2.

_____ 1981. Supreme Court of Canada. *Resolution to Amend the Constitution*, 1 S.C.R. 753 [*Patriation Reference*].

_____ 1982. Supreme Court of Canada. *Reference re Amendment of the Canadian Constitution*, 2 S.C.R. 793.

_____1989. Supreme Court of Canada. YMHA Jewish Community Centre of Winnipeg Inc. v Brown, 1 R.C.S. 1532.

_____ 1991. Supreme Court of Canada. *Renvoi relatif au Régime d'assistance publique du Canada (C.-B.)*, 2 R.C.S. 525.

_____ 1993. Supreme Court of Canada. Finlay v Canada (Ministre des Finances), 1 R.C.S. 108.

_____ 1995. Supreme Court of Canada. RJR-MacDonald Inc. v Canada (Procureur général), 3 R.C.S. 199.

_____ 1997a. Supreme Court of Canada. Eldridge v Colombie-Britannique (Procureur général), 3 R.C.S. 624.

_____ 1997b. Supreme Court of Canada. R. v Hydro-Québec, 3 R.C.S. 213.

_____ 1998. Supreme Court of Canada. Reference re Secession of Quebec, 2 S.C.R. 217.

_____ 2005. Supreme Court of Canada. Chaoulli v Québec (Procureur général),1 R.C.S. 791.0.

Cardinal, Linda 2000. "Le pouvoir exécutif et la judiciarisation de la politique au Canada. Une étude du programme de contestation judiciaire." *Politiques et Sociétés*, 19: 2–3: 43–64.

Cardinal, Linda and Marie-Joie Brady 2007. "Citoyenneté et fédéralisme au Canada : une relation difficile." In *Le fédéralisme canadien contemporain. Fondements, traditions, institutions*, ed. Alain-G. Gagnon. Montreal: Les Presses de l'Université de Montréal, 435–460.

Courchene, Thomas J. 1995. *Célébrer la souplesse: Essai interprétatif sur l'évolution du fédéralisme canadien*. Toronto: C.D. Howe Institute.

Croisat, Maurice 1995. *Le fédéralisme dans les démocraties contemporaines*, 2nd ed. Paris: Montchrestien.

Delmartino, Frank and Kris Deschouer 1994. "Les fondements du fédéralisme." In *Le fédéralisme. Approches politique, économique et juridique*, eds. André Alen et al. Brussels: De Boeck-Wesmael, 9–34.

Delpéré, Francis and Marc Verdussen 2005. "L'égalité, mesure du fédéralisme." In *Le fédéralisme dans tous ses États. Gouvernance, identité et méthodologie (The States and Moods of Federalism. Governance, Identity and Methodology)*, eds. Jean-François Gaudreault-Desbiens and Fabien Gélinas. Cowansville, QC: Les Éditions Yvon Blais, 193–208.

Dion, Stéphane 1992. "Explaining Quebec Nationalism." In *The Collapse of Canada?* ed. R. K. Weaver. Washington D.C.: The Brookings Institution, 77–121.

Dion, Stéphane 1994. "Le fédéralisme fortement asymétrique : improbable et indésirable." In *Seeking a New Canadian Partnership—Asymmetrical and Confederal Options*, ed. F. L. Seidle. Montreal: Institute for Research in Public Policy, 133–152.

Dion, Stéphane 1996. "Les avantages d'un Québec fédéré," quoted in Christian Rouillard and François Rocher, "Using the Concept of Deconcentration to Overcome the Centralization / Decentralization Dichotomy: Thoughts on Recent Constitutional and Political Reform." In *Canada: The State of the Federation 1996*, eds. Patrick C. Fafard and Douglas M. Brown. Kingston, ON: Institute of Intergovernmental Relations, 107.

Elazar, Daniel J. 1982 (Fall). "Confederation and Federal Liberty." *Publius*, 12: 4: 1–14.

Elazar, Daniel J. 1994. *Federalism and the Way to Peace*. Kingston, ON: Institute of Intergovernmental Relations, Queen's University.

Fafard, Patrick, François Rocher and Catherine Côté 2010 (January). "The Presence (or lack thereof) of a Federal Culture in Canada: The Views of Canadians." *Regional and Federal Studies*, 20: 1: 19–43.

Frankel, Max 1986. *Federal Theory*. Canberra: Centre for Research on Federal Financial Relations.

Friedrich, Carl 1974. *Limited Government: A Comparison*. Englewood Cliffs, NJ: Prentice-Hall.

Gagnon, Alain-G. 2009. *The Case for Multinational Federalism*. New York: Routledge.

Gow, James Iain 1992. *Introduction à l'administration publique : une approche politique*. Montreal: Gaétan Morin.

Hiebert, Janet L. 1999. "Wrestling with Rights: Judges, Parliament and the Making of Social Policy."*Choices*, 5: 3–32.

Issalys, Pierre and Denis Lemieux 2002. *L'Action gouvernementale. Précis de droit des institutions administratives*, 2nd ed. Cowansville, QC: Éditions Yvon Blais.

Karmis, Dimitrios and Wayne Norman 2005. *Theories of Federalism: a Reader*. New York: Palgrave Macmillan.

Kelly, James B. 2001 (June). "Reconciling Rights and Federalism during Review of the Charter of Rights and Freedoms: The Supreme Court of Canada and the Centralization Thesis, 1982 to 1999." *Canadian Journal of Political Science*, 34: 2: 321–355.

Kelly, Stéphane and Guy Laforest 2004. "Aux sources de la tradition politique. Les travaux en langue française." In *Débats sur la fondation du Canada*, eds. J. Ajzenstat, Paul Romney and William D. Gardner. Quebec: Presses de l'Université Laval, 527–546.

Knopff, Rainer and F. L. Morton 1985. "Nation-Building and the Canadian Charter of Rights and Freedoms." In *Constitutionalism, Citizenship and Society in Canada*, eds. Alan Cairns and Cynthia Williams. Toronto: University of Toronto Press, 133–182.

Kymlicka, Will 2007. "Ethnocultural Diversity in a Liberal State: Making Sense of the Canadian Model(s)." In *Belonging? Diversity Recognition and Shared Citizenship in Canada*, eds. Keith Banting, Thomas C. Courchene and F. L. Seidle. Montreal: Institute for Research on Public Policy, 1–48.

Laforest, Guy 1992. "La Charte canadienne des droits et libertés au Québec : nationalisme injuste et illégitime." In *Bilan québécois du fédéralisme canadien*, ed. François Rocher. Montreal: VLB, 124–151.

Laforest, Guy 2008 (June). "La Commission Bouchard-Taylor et la place du Québec dans la trajectoire de l'État-nation moderne." At the Conference presented at the IIIrd World Forum on Human Rights: "Gestion démocratique de la diversité culturelle et nationale," Bilbao.

Lajoie, Andrée 2005 (Winter). "Le fédéralisme canadien : science politique fiction pour l'Europe?" *Lex Electronica*, 10: 1: 1–23.

Lajoie, Andrée 2008 (Spring). "Current Exercises of The Federal Spending Power: What Does the Constitutions Say About It?" *Queen's Law Journal*, 34: 1: 141–161.

Lamontagne, M. 1954. *Le fédéralisme canadien : évolution et problèmes*. Quebec: Les Presses de l'Université Laval.

Lazar, Harvey 2008 (Spring). "The Spending Power and the Harper Government." *Queen's Law Journal*, 34: 1: 125–140.

Leclair, Jean 2007. "Vers une pensée politique fédérale : la répudiation du mythe de la différence québécoise 'radicale'." In *Reconquérir le Canada. Un nouveau projet pour la nation québécoise*, ed. Andrée Pratte. Montreal: Les Éditions Vox Parallèles, 39–84.

Leslie, P. M. 1993. "The Fiscal Crisis of Canadian Federalism." In *A Partnership in Trouble—Renegotiating Fiscal Federalism*, eds. P. M. Leslie, K. Norrie and I. K. Ip. Toronto: C. D. Howe Institute, 1–86.

Liquidators of the Maritime Bank of Canada v Receiver-General of New-Brunswick, [1892] A.C. 437, 441–442. In *Re The Initiative and Referendum Act*, (1919), A.C. 935, 942.

Livingston, William S. 1952 (March). "A Note on the Nature of Federalism." *Political Science Quarterly*, 67: 1: 81–95.

Macdougall, J. N. 1991. "The Context For Future Constitutional Options." In *Options for a New Canada*, eds. Ronald L. Watts and D. M. Brown. Toronto: University of Toronto Press.

Mendes, Eroll 2008 (Spring). "Building Firewalls and Deconstructing Canada by Hobbling the Federal Spending Power: The Rise of the Harper Doctrine." *Queens Law Journal*, 34: 1: 225–247.

Mercier, Jean 2004. *L'administration publique. De l'école classique au nouveau management public*, 3rd edition. Montreal: Les Presses de l'Université Laval.

Paquin, Stéphane 2005. "La paradiplomatie identitaire. Le Québec, la Flandre et la Catalogne en relations internationales." *Politique et sociétés*, 23: 176–194.

Pelletier, Benoît ed. 2001. "Comité spécial du Parti libéral du Québec sur l'avenir politique et constitutionnel de la société québécoise. " In *Un Projet pour le Québec. Affirmation, autonomie, leadership*. Montréal: Parti libéral du Québec.

Pelletier, Benoît 2004. "Remise en question des fondements du pouvoir fédéral de dépenser." Speech delivered at the Conference on Economic Redistribution in the Canadian Federation, Toronto: Faculty of Law, University of Toronto, February 6.

Pelletier, Benoît 2006. "Le défi de l'équilibre : les processus de centralisation et de décentralisation dans l'État fédéral canadien." In *La mise en œuvre de la décentralisation : Étude comparée France, Belgique, Canada*, ed. Gilles Guiheux. Actes du Colloque de la Faculté de Droit et de Science politique de Rennes, 18 et 19 novembre 2004. Bruxelles : Bruylant & GDJ, 49–64.

Pelletier, Réjean 2008. *Le Québec et le fédéralisme canadien. Un regard critique.* Sainte-Foy: Les Presses de l'Université Laval.

Quebec 1956, *Report of the Royal Commission of Inquiry on Constitutional Problems*, 2 volumes. (Tremblay Commission). Quebec City [s.n.] Montreal.

Rocher, François and Christian Rouillard 1996 (November). "Using the Concept of Deconcentration to overcome the Centralization/ Decentralization Dichotomy: Thoughts on Recent Constitutional and Political Reform." In *Canada: The State of the Federation 1996*, eds. Patrick C. Fafard and Douglas Brown. Kingston, ON: Institute of Intergovernmental Relations, 99–134.

Rocher, François and Christian Rouillard 1998 (June). "Décentralisation, subsidiarité et néo-libéralisme : quand l'arbre cache la forêt." *Canadian Public Policy / Analyse de politiques*, 24: 2: 233–258.

Rocher, François 2009a. "The Quebec-Canada Dynamic or the Negation of the Ideal of Federalism." In *Contemporary Canadian Federalism.*

Foundations, Traditions, Institutions, ed. Alain-G. Gagnon. Toronto: University of Toronto Press, 81–131

Rocher, François 2009b. "L'avenir de la fédération, l'avenir du fédéralisme : deux enjeux distincts." In *Le fédéralisme en Belgique et au Canada. Comparaison sociopolitique,* eds. Bernard Fournier and Min Reuchamps. Bruxelles: Deboeck, 231–254.

Smiley, Donald V. 1984 (Winter). "Public Sector Politics, Modernization and Federalism: The Canadian American Experience." *Publius,* 14: 1: 39–59.

Stevenson, Garth 2004. *Unfulfilled Union. Canadian Federalism and National Unity,* 4th edition. Montreal and Kingston, ON: McGill-Queens's University Press.

Théret, Bruno 2005. "Du principe fédéral à une typologie des fédérations : quelques propositions." In *Le fédéralisme dans tous ses États. Gouvernance identité et mythologie,* eds. Jean-François Gaudreault-Desbiens and Fabien Gélinas. Cowansville, QC: Les Éditions Yvon Blais, 99–133.

Tully, James 1995a. *Strange Multiplicity. Constitutionalism in an Age of Diversity.* Cambridge, UK: Cambridge University Press.

Tully, James 1995b. *Let's Talk. The Quebec Referendum and The Future of Canada,* paper presented at the Austin and Hempel Lectures, Dalhousie University, March 23.

Valaskakis, Kimon and Angeline Fournier 1995. *Le piège de l'indépendance. Le Québec sera-t-il affaibli par la souveraineté?* Montreal: L'Étincelle.

Wallner, Jennifer 2008. "Empirical Evidence and Pragmatic Explanations: Canada's Contributions to Comparative Federalism." In *The Comparative Turn in Canadian Political Science,* ed. Robert Vipond. Vancouver: UBC Press, 158–176.

Watts, Ronald L. 1999a. *Comparing Federal Systems.* 2nd edition. Montreal and Kinston, ON: McGill-Queen's University Press.

Watts, Ronald L. 1999b. *The Spending Power in Federal Systems: A Comparative Study.* Kingston, ON: Institute of Intergovernmental Relations.

Weinstock, Daniel M. 2001. "Vers une théorie normative du fédéralisme." *Revue internationale des sciences sociales,* 1: 167 : 79–87.

Wheare, K. C. 1963. *Federal Government.* 4e edition. London, UK: Oxford University Press.

Wheare, K. C. 1996, cited in *The Moral Foundations of Canadian Federalism. Paradoxes, Achievements, and Tragedy of Nationhood,* by Samuel La Selva. Montreal and Kingston, ON: McGill-Queen's University Press, 30.

Woehrling, José 2009. "The Canadian Charter of Rights and Freedoms and Its Consequences for Political and Democratic Life and the Federal System." In *Contemporary Canadian Federalism. Foundations, Traditions, Institutions,* ed. Alain-G. Gagnon. Toronto: University of Toronto Press, 224–249.

Chapter 6

Toward an
Autopoietic Federalism

Ruth Hubbard and Gilles Paquet

> *A system is autopoietic when its function is primarily geared to self-renewal.*
>
> —Erich Jantsch

Introduction

In democratic confederal systems, the debate about centralization and decentralization is a debate about means—about different ways in which a particular governance regime might crystallize structurally, arguing in favour of one form over the other. But such a discussion makes little sense unless one can identify, ever so loosely, the long-run objective being pursued—not the precise end products that are sought, but the process one wishes to sustain.

Federalism is a collaborative governance regime that is attempting to respond to the heterogeneous challenges of pluralistic, rapidly evolving environments. It is an amalgam of structures, processes and mechanisms that are meant to generate both the requisite amount of coordination to deal effectively with the variety of citizens' demands as well as a timely capacity to transform (through social learning) in the face of changing environments and/or evolving priorities (Paquet 1977, 2005: chapter 13).

In the public sector governance world, the last half-century has brought a slight centralization-to-decentralization drift; one that has been bemoaned by some and celebrated by others. A parallel evolution in private sector governance has seen the emergence of hybrid organizational forms pioneered by concerns like Benetton, that have transformed their production process away from a focus on vertical control and economies of scale (the V form) toward one (the H form) geared to horizontal and transversal networking, which generates flexibility and variety at low costs in the face of significant and ongoing change, while maintaining and even improving quality and self-renewal.

Our hypothesis is that this drift ought to be welcomed for two reasons. First, it is clear that only by devolving decision making to local arenas is there any likelihood that a differentiated population (with diverse views about the nature of 'the good') can hope to receive public goods and services in keeping with its diverse preferences. Second, because of the polycentric nature of their governance, decentralized arrangements are more likely to generate the necessary experimentation as well as the essential quick learning of new means and ends.

However logical it may be, this argument is unlikely to be persuasive unless a strategy aimed at reinforcing this drift can be shown to be technically feasible, socially acceptable, implementable, and not too politically destabilizing (Taylor 1997). Indeed, it has been the main counter-argument of the phalanx of centralizers that decentralization may be theoretically desirable but it is unworkable in practice. In fact, for most centralizers, the only choice is between centralization and chaos.

In this chapter we proceed in five stages. First, we examine the general organizational drift from Big G (Government) to small g (governance) triggered by the need to provide variety, flexibility and fast social learning at low cost. Second, we identify major blockages that have slowed the process of social learning underpinning this evolution, and some ways in which they can be overcome. Third, we take notice, succinctly, of attacks on decentralization that argue it is unworkable, overly costly and inequitable (among other things), and show these criticisms to be ill founded. Fourth, we sketch four plausible scenarios for the future of Canadian federalism and argue for open-source federalism (i.e., less state centricity, more collaboration and generalized inclusion) as the most promising possibility. Fifth, we identify some prerequisites for this vibrantly decentralized federalism scenario to become seen as a preferred alternative, and some of the virtuous scheming that will be necessary to launch such a Canadian *perestroika*.

From G to g

It has been suggested by Daniel Innerarity (quoting an apocryphal Sigmund Freud) that there are three impossible professions (to educate, to cure and to govern): in each case, success requires some sort of collaboration of the parties who, at first sight, would appear to be passive beneficiaries (Innerarity 2006: 193). This is certainly true about governance. Public governance and its circumstances in most democracies are complex adaptive systems like the human central nervous system or immune system, or an ecosystem, and operate the same way. The human immune system includes a brigade of antibodies that fight and destroy an ever-changing cast of invading bacteria and viruses of such variety that the system must continually learn, adapt, improvise and overcome. The central nervous system contains hundreds of millions of neurons, interacting, combining and recombining in different patterns to deal with a complex and ever-changing context; it has a continually renewed ability to cope, anticipate, adapt and learn (Holland 1995).

Similarly, public governance and its circumstances are made up of a large number of actors, relationships, routines, norms and mindsets that are in a constant process of evolution in the face of the challenges of the day.

Such a system has certain characteristics.

First, it is 'open', i.e., it receives material and non-material resources from the external environment, and it is shaped to a degree by its environment. As a whole, it is like a living organism, capable of scanning the context and of managing its interdependence with its environment.

Second, because it is open, this kind of system must 'adapt' to its environment, (i.e., modify its social and technical texture in response to the changes in the environment) if it wishes to maintain a certain 'goodness of fit' with the context, so as to be 'adopted' by the environment in turn (i.e., to have a higher probability of survival and prosperity). In the case of a public socio-technical system, a higher degree of goodness of fit with its context generates high performance, while misfits produce lower performance levels—thriving or surviving.

Third, it must be sensitive to what is occurring in the world beyond in terms both of space and time, and modify its technologies, its processes and its structures in an effort to respond strategically and effectively to the environment. This entails a process of 'differentiation' of the system to respond to the different challenges posed by the environment.

Fourth, it is a complex system in which the 'interactions' among the individuals and their organizations generate a dynamic of their own. Every agent is forced to define strategies to react to the actions of other agents. Agents must adapt and discover new rules and new behaviors that generate the requisite 'coordination and integration' for high performances to ensue for the system as a system.

In other words, the public sector as a 'complex adaptive system' is a set of ongoing relationships between people and organizations, governed by reactions to the environment and by mutual expectations. It has become differentiated and integrated in a particular manner over time, and its governance has had to evolve accordingly: to enable the system to maintain itself—to grow and to innovate—governance must be as varied and diverse as the environment and the interactions it is trying to deal with. This is the "law of requisite variety" (Ashby 1956): the capacity of a system to evolve and learn effectively (i.e., to govern itself in an effective manner) depends on its capacity to move to more complex forms of differentiation and integration, to be able to deal with the variety of challenges and opportunities in novel ways, and to maintain its coherence through time while retaining some characteristics that are sources of good fits and shedding some that are sources of misfits. In today's fast-paced, globalized world, this demands effective social learning.

The drift from state-centric governing

Over the last few decades, there has been a shift from state-centric governing towards arrangements that give greater valence not only to the private and social sectors but also to junior levels of government and smaller units in general. The situation is best captured by Naisbitt's *Global Paradox*: the bigger the world economy, the more powerful its smallest players. The idea that the central government is the most important part of governance is becoming obsolete. New forms of polycentric governance are emerging as more important because they are more effective at generating timely responses (Naisbitt 1994: 51).

The meaning of this drift from Big G (Government) to small g (governance) is best explained with reference to table 6.1.

In Canada, the drift was not the result of a deliberate change in philosophy (even though such a shift has materialized over time), but of chronic public deficits that forced the central government to restructure its operations.

Table 6.1   The drift from G to g

	DRIFT	
	G	g
Key Characteristics	Public sector ≥ (better than) private	Private sector ≥ (better than) public
	Redistribution on the basis of rights	Redistribution on the basis of needs
	Soft egalitarianism	Subsidiarity
	Centralization	Decentralization

Beginning with the creation of Canada in the late 19th century, it was assumed that the public sector was able to perform better than the private sector (and the central 'headquarters' better than the local ones in all sectors) in tackling the challenges of the country. From the late 1970s on, doubts began to creep in about it (Paquet 1997). But it was not until the 1990s, when the Canadian fiscal situation had deteriorated sufficiently for it to become thinkable that the IMF (International Monetary Fund) might be forced to impose some discipline, that the Chrétien government was forced to review, systematically, what the citizens could legitimately expect from the state. This exercise is often referred to as 'program review', and led to a significant drift from government (G) to governance (g) (Paquet 1999).

Although this action was mainly inspired by fiscal pressures, a philosophy of subsidiarity became the guidepost, calling both for a new division of labour among sectors (private, public, social) and a drive towards devolution of responsibility (within the public sector and across sector boundaries). Wealth creation concerns came to carry more weight than its distribution, so the case for state-centrism and centralization (because massive redistribution requires bringing the loot to the centre first) weakened. In Canada, soft egalitarianism, enforced as a matter of right, gave way to a new consensus on 'equability': on redistribution only to the extent that needs required it, and that politically unacceptable inequality called for corrective action.

The new division of labour among sectors entailed the abandonment of the old sharp division between the public and the private sectors as many new forms of mixed organization proved more efficient. Indeed, one might regard the Jane Jacobs book of the early 1990s (Jacobs 1992) as the last stand of those for whom any mixing of the private and public sectors could only lead to "monstrous hybrids". *De facto*, it became the new norm that various forms of partnership between sectors could better achieve the efficiency and equity goals that were jointly sought (Goldsmith and Eggers 2004).

Government also gradually realized that, in order to be effective, meso-level actions were required. This has led to a corresponding deconstruction of the public sector into new units that are more local (city-regions) and more-clearly aligned with communities of practice (that crystallize within and around issue domains or arenas). These units of analysis emerged as basic building blocks where individual practitioners (the professional realm), domains (skills, practices, rules), fields (kinds of expertise), and the interest of other stakeholders (consumers, citizens, business executives, etc.) were more likely to be well aligned. In certain arenas, the appropriate level for aggregating communities of practice proved to be at the federal or provincial levels, but there was a growing likelihood in many sectors that smaller or more diffuse building blocks, arranged in baroque ways, could produce better results (Gardner et al. 2001; Wenger et al. 2002).

The centrality of ligatures

The system of governance in good currency in Canada is a complex and fuzzy palimpsest of layers of formal and informal arrangements accumulated over time as new rules have come to be written over old ones. Any interventions in this script always disturb the delicate and fragile equilibria in the mix of structure-theory-technology that makes up this social system: the structure of roles and relations among individuals, the theory/views held within the system about its purposes, operations, environment and future, and the prevailing technology of the system all hang together, so that any change in one produces change in the others (Schön 1971: 33). Poor performance is often ascribable to a poor alignment between the perspectives of the different stakeholders or between theory/structure/technology.

Given that the structures and roles of a system and the 'theory-in-use' are much more deeply embedded sub-systems than technology, effective interventions may work better through engineering new mechanisms that may help it achieve its social learning potential, rather than by trying to change structure or theory. The vested interests in the technologies are less likely to unleash the full force of strong dynamic conservatism.

There is also a need for inter-domain coherence to be ensured by adequate ligatures that reinforce the underlying institutional order. The multiple logics at play in different issue domains or arenas generate spillover effects onto others. The degree to which taboos might exist in one sector is bound to limit what can be done in another. But the emergence of new mechanisms in one domain (like users' fees) is bound not only to affect the structure of roles and the theory of what business one is in within that domain, but also to have some reverberation on related issue domains.

Ligatures are also quite important at the cognitive level. They establish a corridor within which one may experiment safely. This is the sense in which the reference points constituted by 'the welfare state' for instance (with its focus on security and entitlements as a matter of right but also with its priority to redistribution over wealth creation and its anti-growth and anti-efficiency bias) has served as a key nexus of ligatures for the old institutional order.

Mechanisms and ligatures are in the process of changing in democracies around the world, including in Canada, and are crystallizing around the new reference point we have called "the strategic state" at the core of small g governance (Paquet 1996–7). This has dramatically changed the valence of the public sector implying significant change in the structure and functioning of public administration.

Major social learning blockages

Canadian well-being is the result of the success or lack of it in organizing, instituting and governing in ways that have a high yield in economic, political and social terms. Such coordination and governance may take many forms and shapes—mixing top-down hierarchical coercion, horizontal exchange relations, relationships based on solidarity, and bottom-up self-organizing processes generating a sense of direction from below. Federalism as a mind-set allows for this fluidity and variability and, as a result, fosters the design of a public sector and its circumstances that are likely to promote a greater degree of effective social learning—a necessity today.

To catalyze social learning in complex organizations, one must have some view about the ways in which collective intelligence works. Elsewhere, we have very profitably used an approach suggested by Max Boisot (Boisot 1995).

The information space

In an effort to identify the major obstacles to social learning (and therefore to guide corrective interventions), Max Boisot has mapped the social learning cycle in a three-dimensional space—'the information space'—which identifies an organizational system in terms of the degree of 'abstraction, codification and diffusion' of the information flows within it. This three-dimensional space (see figure 6.1) defines three continua: the farther away from the origin on the vertical axis, the more the information is codified (i.e., the more its form is clarified, stylized and simplified); the farther away from the origin laterally eastward, the more widely the information is diffused and shared; and the farther away from the origin laterally westward, the more abstract the information is (i.e., the more general the categories in use).

Figure 6.1   Learning cycle and potential blockages

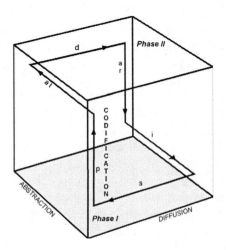

The social learning cycle is presented in two phases with three steps in each phase: phase I emphasizes the cognitive dimensions of the cycle, while phase II deals with the diffusion of the new information.

In Phase I, learning begins with some scanning of the environment, and of the concrete information widely diffused and known, in order to detect anomalies and paradoxes. Following this first step (s), one is led in step 2 to stylize the problem (p) posed by the anomalies and paradoxes in a language of problem solution; the third step of phase I purports to generalize the solution found to the more specific issue to a broader family of problems through a process of abstraction (at). In Phase II, the new knowledge is diffused (d) to a larger community of persons or groups in step 4. There is then a process of absorption (ar) of this new knowledge by the population, and its assimilation so as to become part of the tacit stock of knowledge in step 5. In step 6, the new knowledge is not only absorbed, but has an impact (i) on the concrete practices and artifacts of the group or community.

In figure 6.1, one may identify the different blockages through the learning cycle: in Phase I, cognitive dissonance in (s) may prevent the anomalies from being noted; epistemic inhibitions of all sorts in (p) may stop the process of translation into a language of problem solution; blockages preventing the generalization of the new knowledge because of the problem definition being encapsulated within the here and now (at) may keep the new knowledge from acquiring the most effective degree of generality. In Phase II, the new knowledge may not get the appropriate diffusion because of property rights (d), or because of certain values or very strong dynamic conservatism which may generate a refusal to listen by those most likely to profit from the new knowledge (ar), or because of difficulties in finding ways to incorporate the new knowledge (i).

Interventions to remove or attenuate the negative effects of such blockages always entail some degree of interference with the mechanisms of collective intelligence. In some cases, such as the modification of property rights, the changes in the rules appear relatively innocuous, even though government interferes significantly in the affairs of the mind: correcting social learning blockages modifies relational transactions, and therefore the psychosocial fabric of the organization.

Learning blockages

In the case of liberal democratic societies (and in the case of federal systems in particular), there are inherent blockages in each of the two phases.

The first kind of blockage is at the epistemic level.

Citizens have increasingly ceased to regard the state as omnipotent and benign. As a result, they have asked to be more involved in both policy development and program design, as well as to have access to the levers required to change organizational or institutional behavior. This has rendered the process of collective learning considerably more cacophonous. This, in turn, has meant a greater difficulty in creating the requisite forums and agoras for deliberation, significantly slowed down the process of aggregation of preferences, and mitigated the capacity to distil a dominant view about many of the anomalies. In this way, both the processes of codification and abstraction have been greatly impaired in recent times in these societies. To this must be added the obfuscation and confusion that is often sewn by irresponsible and ideologically anchored media.

For federal states, there is an additional complexity because two or more orders of government share *sovereign* authority—something that adds to the numbers of players and consequently generates somewhat greater coordination challenges to overcome. In the case of Canadian federalism, a further impediment can stem from a mix of cultural factors (a certain trust in authority and dislike of conflict), the congenital arrogance of the federal government, and the often unenlightened competitiveness of other orders of government. This has often led to both a heightening of natural tensions and to some cognitive dissonance and ambivalence on the part of citizens bombarded by contradictory messages.

For example, the federal government, in Canada (and elsewhere), has been often described as "(using its power) ...in a way that creates a single, nation-wide community with shared values and shared, enforceable understandings of how local communities of all descriptions should be organized" (Carter 1998: 19). This 'anti-democratic' and 'anti-communitarian', top-down approach has led to much cognitive dissonance: the whole debate about fiscal imbalance in Canada is a good illustration of this cognitive blockage (Paquet 2004).

The second kind of blockage is at the diffusion level, where collaboration is again mandatory for effectiveness.

While by definition, federalism as a formal system should be better able to serve a pluralistic and deeply diverse citizenry more appropriately than in a unitary one (which is why it was invented), in today's world, the multiplication of levels of governing, the extent of local patriotism, and the existence of a wide variety of different interests and values can make the diffusion of particularly helpful responses to generic problems more difficult than might otherwise be the case.

Canada's brand of competitive formal federalism has proved capable of generating confusion and action overlap, and of allowing counterproductive adversarialism to inhibit collaboration in a significant way. The collaboration and partnering that are needed entail power sharing, and are often regarded as unacceptable in principle by the very organizations claiming to want to partner (Paquet 2001). The recent antics of Newfoundland's Premier Danny Williams and of federalist leaders in Quebec have shown how inflammatory populist rhetoric can easily trump political rationality. So in difficult times, when the amount and kind of collaboration required are deeper and richer than before, and there is a need for a greater variety of forums, reporting standards, and collaborative structures of a more permanent sort, these essential elements are often simply not there or not used.

It is clear that some 'bricolage' is in order: the social learning apparatus needs to be repaired and enriched if decentralized governance is to be as effective as it can be. But it does not mean in any way that the decentralization strategy is unworkable or ineffective because the existing institutional basis is deficient in certain ways and requires some institutional makeover.

The case for bricolage

One may divide the array of mechanisms through which one may intervene in the social learning cycle into four broad families corresponding to the portion of the system to be catalyzed. On the cognitive side, information together with forums and reporting are meant to ginger up Phase I of the social learning cycle; on the diffusion/dissemination side, one is looking at mechanisms to generate trust and fail-safe mechanisms in order to strengthen Phase II. While these mechanisms may not be sufficient to ensure optimal functioning, they would appear to be at least necessary to make decentralized arrangements workable.

Getting rid of inhibitions in the cognitive sub-cycle

Collective intelligence is based on a capacity for all the stakeholders to work cooperatively in detecting anomalies, codifying them and generalizing the findings to a broader family of issues. It requires three things: (1) a modicum of timely and credible information on which the different parties or groups may base their provisional judgment about the state of affairs; (2) a locus (real or virtual) for stakeholders to work at reconciling their viewpoints, working through their relations with each other, and learning from each other (Yankelovich and Rosell 2000); and (3) the basic conditions for sustainable partnerships: ensuring that all parties gain from the arrangement, and that each party is likely to honor its obligations even when that is not necessarily the preferred option (Sacconi 2000).

An uninformed or a misinformed agent is unable to develop an appreciation of the situation and can be easily manipulated into taking a stand that can only lead to his/her not achieving the best possible level of knowledge and well-being. And it cannot be presumed that the required information will materialize by 'immaculate conception'. Consequently, it is crucial to ensure that the modicum of timely and credible information is available and accessible for agents to be able to make reasonable decisions. This is the rationale for the existence of public agencies like Statistics Canada, but there are also private and not-for-profit agencies that have emerged to perform similar functions.

In many sectors and domains, like health, the relevant comparable indicators have not been available until very recently, and are still far from completely satisfactory. In education, opacity remains the rule. It is therefore of prime importance to ensure that, in issue domains where intervention would appear to be required, the basic usable facts are not only recorded but made available to the citizenry. Nothing destroys the effectiveness of nonsensical rants or toxic lies more effectively than a modicum of information appropriately explained to the citizens (Paquet 2009a, 2009b).

Another key family of missing mechanisms has to do with 'forums' for dialogue and multilogue. Even though there may be a fair understanding of the rationale for partnering, and an appreciation of the different structures and roles that would be useful, in many cases, the barriers to partnering are often ascribable to the lack of a locus where the different parties can meet, deliberate and negotiate.

A good example is the issue of fiscal imbalance between the federal, provincial and local governments. This calls for fiscal 'concertation', but there is no place where the three parties can meaningfully meet and negotiate. While it might have been expected that the Council of the Federation (where provincial and territorial leaders meet) could serve this purpose, the fact that the federal government and the big municipalities have been explicitly excluded is bound to have a stunting effect on the whole process of deliberation.

For collective intelligence to develop, effective feedback is crucial. Consequently, there must be feedback if there is to be accountability, learning and behavior adjustment in response to context and other stakeholders. In a game without a master, agents face constant tradeoffs among a multitude of *de facto* vertical, horizontal and transversal accountabilities, and not just the traditional financial one. Such accountabilities are embodied in moral contracts with all other meaningful stakeholders that can only be couched in the most general terms, but they need to be binding in order to be meaningful.

Therefore, another key family of missing mechanisms is 'reporting'. The lack of quick and clear feedback reports means that there is no strong learning loop. While adding a reporting mechanism in no way pre-directs the outcome, it ensures that there will be learning and heightened collective intelligence. New techniques of collective reporting may not only generate a heightened degree of collective intelligence but also may have a significant impact on dissemination of effective responses and trigger new modes of collaboration. Indeed, it may lead to the crystallization of an issue domain that serves as a focal point for multiple stakeholders.

Honouring of obligations is the Achilles' heel of this phase of the social learning cycle. The Social Union Framework Agreement mentioned in Peach's chapter and a number of arrangements in the Far North that have failed to evolve smoothly with circumstances, provide clear evidence of the difficulties. In the former case, the dominant partner (in this case the federal government) would have needed to resist the temptation to deceive its partner(s) about its real commitment to the partnership's goals—which it clearly did not. In the latter case, the lack of explicit mechanisms to adjust as smoothly as possible to predictably evolving circumstances has proved lethal a number of times.

In both cases, a degree of reporting to the public at large would tend to reduce the temptation to enter disingenuously into 'pseudo-partnerships' as well as to foster more realistic and less fundamentalist assumptions about what a specific partnership can actually reasonably achieve when the ground is in motion.

Getting rid of blockages in the diffusion sub-cycle
The diffusion sub-cycle depends first and foremost on stewardship and trust. It requires a capacity for listening and the

open-mindedness of all parties to overcome the rivalry and envy that threatens cooperation (O'Toole 1995).

First, we need to think differently about stewardship. Traditionally, there has been a tendency to count on super-bureaucrats or "delta bureaucrats" à la Dror (1997) or the judiciary to provide the lead when the different stakeholders appear unable to come to terms about a general direction for action. This is potentially dangerous in today's world because presuming the 'necessity' of top-down and centralized decision making undercuts the possibility of any stewardship emerging from the creativity of partners. It is a holdover from the outmoded state-centric view of the world.

James O'Toole has proposed a different view. For him, the leader's ability to lead is a by-product of the trust he has earned by serving his followers. The burden of office of the leader is to "refine the public views in a way that transcends the surface noise of pettiness, contradiction and self interest" (O'Toole 1995: 10–12). This view of leadership suggests that impasses may indeed be overcome by the stakeholders themselves.

The key family of mechanisms to refurbish trust is not, as usually assumed, strictly focused on stratagems to reduce secrecy or increase transparency. "Demands for universal transparency are likely to encourage the evasions, hypocrisies and half-truths that we usually refer to as 'political correctness,' but which might more forthrightly be called 'self-censorship' or 'deception'" (O'Neill 2002: 73).

One should therefore focus on deception—the real culprit in reducing trust—and transparency does little to reduce deception. What is needed is a family of 'mechanisms to reduce deception, evasion and outright lies'. This can be done in large measure by rejecting politically correct vocabulary, by refusing to endorse slogans, half-truths and complicity with them, and by insisting on an active view of citizenship based on duties, not rights (Ibid., 37–38).

But most importantly, this will emerge from the development of "trust systems" that are made of mechanisms to help transfer trust from individuals to the system as a whole (Thuderoz et al. 1999). For instance, in the race for greater external transparency in internal audit reports, there is inevitable sanitizing of results in order to minimize blaming. This trumps clear talking about possible improvements. At the level of parliamentary scrutiny, the emphasis on financial accountability, without an equivalent focus on performance, can entail a signal that doing something the right way is more important than doing the right thing. In a world in which one wants to encourage learning and not simply blaming, incentives and sanctions matter and are an important part of trustful systems.

Development of such systems has proved to be immensely easier to accomplish at the meso-level, where issue domains are broad but limited enough to ensure that communities of practice can conveniently meet, meaningfully deliberate, and generate workable arrangements or promising experiments with reasonably effective incentives and sanctions in place. While it may be impossible to create a trust system about the whole of the health field, it may be thinkable to develop one in dealing with mental health. In such a more circumscribed world, domain, field, community of practice and stakeholders interests are likely to be better aligned, a steady diet of conflicts happily resolved, and elements of trust being allowed to emerge.

However, it would be naive to assume that there will be no opportunism. As a result, a residual threat is required: the threat that, if cooperation does not prevail, an outcome that no one desires might ensue. This is why the family of 'fail-safe or default mechanisms' is so powerful: in effect a knife is being put to the throat of the negotiators, thus creating the right incentive reward system to act in good faith. When fail-safe mechanisms or default mechanisms are in place, inaction is not an option and sabotage is discouraged. When parties fail to come up with a collaborative answer, every one is aware that the fail-safe mechanism kicks in.

These fail-safe mechanisms might be 'quasi-markets', binding referenda, earmarked taxes, or other devices that empower the citizenry and the users, and reduce the margin of arbitrariness that officials (in the private, public and social sectors, governors and managers) may enjoy: citizens are not pawns in the hands of knights in this new world of small g governance, but queens attempting to deal effectively with knaves. The fail-safe mechanisms induce elected and un-elected officials to act more like knights than knaves (Le Grand 2003).

Decentralized federalism and its enemies

Despite the plausibility of the decentralization strategy being the preferable option (if the major blockages are removed or attenuated), it has been sufficient for those in denial *vis-à-vis* the drift from the welfare state to the strategic state (Hubbard and Paquet 2007) to simply claim that whatever may be argued at the conceptual level in favour of decentralization is unlikely to work in practice. This tactic is often based on anecdotal evidence and has been used very widely to infer, without further consideration, that centralization is mandatory.

In this section, we propose to deal succinctly with a few of those attacks on decentralized federalism that are purported to be deadly.

Lack of capacity and competence of the citizenry

This first attack is based on the presumed expertise at the centre and the presumed incompetence of the citizenry, but also of lower order governments and of private and social concerns. It is tantamount to an epistemological *coup d'état* by senior governments: the claimed technical expertise at the centre is said to be sufficient to banish all other parties to the role of lobbies of all sorts—agents that have opinions and preferences but no moral authority or adequate expertise to legitimately and properly assess the situation and to decide on the 'called for' action. This is a form of cognitive despotism that attempts to substitute a certain self-legitimizing claim to expertise and a certain auto-declaration of infallibility to replace the intellectual resources by which people grant or withhold legitimacy.

This argument may be countered in many ways. One may use the most interesting result in modern social theory: the Condorcet Jury Theorem that the probability of a majority of a group being right increases toward 100 percent as the size of the group increases, providing that the probability of each voter being correct exceeds 50 percent (Sunstein 2006: 25). This means that the citizens need not be omniscient, but only to be more likely than not to give the right answer, for bottom-up participatory processes to succeed. There has also been a substantial body of empirical evidence accumulated that demonstrates that mass collaboration is not only possible but effective (Surowiecki 2004; Tapscott and Williams 2006; Shirky 2008). So it cannot be argued meaningfully that mass collaboration cannot work.

There is no doubt that accessible, timely and credible information is necessary if mass collaboration is to succeed, and that some cognitive infrastructure has to be in place to ensure that collaboration is based on a sound information base (Paquet 2009a: chapter 4). However there is no reason that such cognitive infrastructure cannot be effectively created at the local or interprovincial level or that such decentralized infrastructure is of necessity less efficient than the centralized version. Indeed, the reverse is most likely true, as long as it is beyond a certain minimum optimum scale. In any case, there is no reason to presume that capacity and competence can only exist at the top, and that, given the power of appropriate technology, bottom-up governance cannot be effective.

Unworkable, too costly and inequitable
Collaboration, even though it is laudable in theory, is fiendishly difficult in practice. But it does not mean that it is either unworkable or necessarily costly. We now have both many experimental studies and documented case studies that have shown that networked social production and other forms of collaboration are both value-adding and sustainable even in social systems where reciprocators are not the majority (Gintis et al. 2005; Benkler 2006; Tapscott and Williams 2006; Parker and Gallagher 2007).

As for the supposedly high costs of variety and collaboration, they represent some sort of myth ascribable to a mindset still dominated by the drive toward uniformity and economies of scale. One of the most important learnings in industrial organization of the last decade is that variety and differentiation need not be costly as long as appropriate modularization of the production process is ensured (Garud et al. 2003). This is the case as much for a whole range of public goods as for the production of automobiles.

Finally, decentralization obviously allows much differentiation to respond to differences in circumstances and preferences. But departure from uniformity generates unease in those for whom simplistic egalitarianism is the golden rule. Deviation from uniformity, being regarded as a violation of the equality credo, entails a refusal of variety even though it would serve the diverse citizens better and perhaps be more to their liking. In fact, equity does not entail uniformity. And attacks on variety in the name of equity are sheer nonsense.

Consequently, despite the ideological bias against public-private partnerships and other such collaborative arrangements (decreed unworkable) or against differentiation and variety (decreed costly and inequitable), the challenge of serving a pluralistic and heterogeneous citizenry is bound to foster collaborative arrangements generating variety, and this is most likely to result from decentralized arrangements.

Fear of local corruptibility and myopia
One last argument that is broadly used is the fear that a decentralized system is more vulnerable to corruption because it is more likely to allow smaller units to be hijacked by groups planning to make use of the local public assets for private purposes. Undeniably, there is a greater vulnerability to the power being seized by populist local burgomasters *à la* Premier Danny Williams than the same happening at the national level. But there are obviously ways to prevent such developments or to attenuate the toxic effects of such initiatives considerably. Moreover, it is not clear that

immunization from such unfortunate developments is in any way ensured by the sheer presence of centralization.

There has been much evidence of narrow mindedness and myopia in the strategy adopted by some premiers or local leaders on issues of national import. But there have been equally numerous instances of ideologically inspired destructive interventions and stances by federal leaders. The spiteful behavior of the Rt. Hon. Pierre Elliott Trudeau (both as a Prime Minister and in retirement) revealed a capacity to deter collaboration and to sabotage collaborative initiatives (Meech Lake and Charlottetown accords) that remains unparalleled at any other level (Burelle 2005).

The capacity for developing a 'super-vision' (i.e., of operating from the high ground and helping others to gain an appreciation of the broad scene that they would not have achieved alone) (Innerarity 2006: 194) has been demonstrated amply by individuals from all sectors and from all levels of government (Blakeney, Castonguay, Lougheed, etc.). For federal officials to pronounce that such super-vision can only be accessed from the federal state level is groundless and self-serving.

Four scenarios

Even though there has been some evolution from big G to small g in the recent past, and a tendency for more citizen engagement, more mass collaboration, more public-private collaboration and more inter-governmental cooperation, this drift has been erratic, and it has occurred despite much resistance by the federal government. The brand of federalism of the Chrétien-Martin governments of the 1990s and early 2000s has remained state-centric and confrontational, and has been built on the dogma that there is a necessity of maintaining a very robust control of the federation from its Ottawa centre.

Nevertheless, for all the reasons mentioned above, Canadian federalism has been forced to adapt somewhat. Figure 6.2 suggests four scenarios that might be regarded as plausible

Figure 6.2   Four scenarios of Canadian federalism

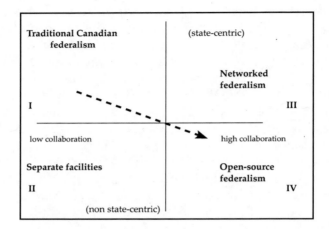

as we look into the future. The least likely scenario is the *status quo* traditional Canadian federalism (I): too much has been noted about its ineffectiveness, and the discontent it is generating for its future to be regarded as satisfactory and likely to persist.

Two sets of forces are pulling the system in different directions: (i) toward less federal state centricity and more power being devolved to sub-national states; this might entail a drift toward a regime of separate facilities (II); and (ii) toward more collaboration as a result of the realization that only collaborative governance might work, but with the constraint that the central state should/must occupy the dominant position at the centre of the stage, i.e., entailing a drift toward regime (III) .

Neither of these two scenarios is very appealing.

The separate facilities scenario is bound to increase the costs of transactions and unlikely to facilitate collaboration.

As for the so-called networked but strongly centric federalism scenario, it has received a good deal of support at the federal level. Still, most discussions of this new form of stewardship (once they are cleansed of their obfuscating rhetoric) would appear to be built on the non-negotiable assumption that the central state must continue to make final decisions even in normal times. This scenario has lost its confederal spirit and is unlikely to provide the degree of flexibility that is considered essential. Central actions since the collapse of the Social Union Framework Agreement have served only to reinforce the non-viability of what now looks like a deceitful accord built on pseudo-consultation and hegemonic power.

Of course, it has always been assumed that, in abnormal or crisis times, some extraordinary state control might/should be invoked, in the same manner that the *War Measures Act* may be invoked in times of crisis. But scenario III would appear to suggest a permanent state of extraordinary central state control—*un état d'exception permanent* (Agamben 2003)—not well aligned to the need for cooperation today.

The big G to small g drift has brought forth a scenario of 'softer paternalism' in some more enlightened countries, but in Canada, top-down autocratic and centralized decision making would appear to have remained in force. Canada's approach remains fundamentally Hegelian: the state (always spelled with a capital S) is regarded as the fundamental societal 'organism', with moral purposes that transcend those of its individual citizens, and it is assumed dogmatically that the central state knows best. Warm offers to collaborate (*du bout des lèvres*) is never meant in Canada to challenge the hyper-centralization-driven federal state, because, as we said earlier, without such centralization ensuring that the loot is brought to the centre, there cannot be the massive redistribution which remains a dominant concern and power lever of the federal state. The resilience of this centralized mindset has been amply demonstrated by its persistence even under Conservative (formerly Progressive Conservative) governments, and cannot be ascribed only to the current global economic crisis.

Scenario IV opens the possibility of escaping from both these traps: it emphasizes the possibility of reducing state centricity through allowing individuals, other groups, and/ or lower order governments to take on a greater role in the name of subsidiarity, while emphasizing the centrality of mass collaboration. It is built on the premise that one does not need to rely exclusively on credentialed stewards (e.g., politicians and bureaucrats) in charge to generate collaboration. Wikipedia, Linux and VISA have clearly shown that coordination can emerge in other ways.

In this scenario IV, Canadian federalism is 'open source federalism': the state no longer occupies centre stage: (i) the people's will and ability to shape their own destiny are the main drivers; (ii) like in other open-source experiments, prototyping and serious play are of central importance (Schrage 2000); and (iii), in this regime, geared to promote growth, productivity and innovation, the role of the state would focus on the removal of the major sources of 'unfreedoms' rather than on regimentation.

Open source federalism would entail a significant amount of experimentation, and the acceptance that experiments will differ from sector/region to sector/region, and will often fail. The guidepost in such experimentation, therefore, cannot be instant success, but minimum regret. Governance and stewardship failures cannot be corrected by simply adding on mechanical contraptions. In the end, some reframing and some cultural change would be required.

We believe that this last scenario, while risky, is the most interesting one.

Key to the evolution in this direction is (1) a drift toward a form of federalism that, to the greatest extent possible, enables each citizen and group of citizens to have access to the 'code' and to tinker freely with the way the stewardship system works within certain well-accepted constraints; and (2) a priority given to 'serious play' (i.e., the development of a premium on innovation and experimentation with the view that, if experimentation is encouraged, necessary retooling, restructuring and reframing are more likely to occur innovatively and productively). The state would remain the backstop in extraordinary circumstances.

Janice Stein has written an important excursus on open source networks in her 2006 essay on federalism. Open source is for Stein "a story of the governance of shared space" (Stein 2006: 47). Boldly, Stein leaps from her short history of open source to the future of Canadian federalism. One might have expected her to develop her argument in the direction of scenario IV, but unfortunately she did not. She erred on the side of caution. On the one hand, she explicitly states that network federalism and shared policy space are not meant to replace the existing legal and institutional order that govern federalism; on the other hand, she does not restrict their ambit to overlapping jurisdictions and even mentions that "officials from governments and other relevant institutions" (Ibid., 52) should partake in the evaluation of policy "after it was rolled out".

But the cautious, tentative and somewhat nebulous nature of the Stein proposal (that constitutes only a few pages at the end of her essay) leaves it unclear how far she is willing to go in allowing the open source process to come fully into play—i.e., to allow all interested parties and not only officials to have access to the code and to tinker with the governing process. One senses that, despite the occasional turns of phrase that would appear to hint at a true open source process, the shadow of state-centricity-cum-focus-on-select-elites is omnipresent. Consequently, it is a state apparatus and a select group of leaders that are called to the table, and not, as in true open source spirit, the whole community of 'hackers'.

Despite the tiptoeing that leads one to surmise that Stein is really veering toward scenario III as the sort of future of federalism she prefers, there are elements in her presentation that entice the reader (and most certainly the authors of this chapter) to carry her suggestions a step further, and to propose a more ambitious program that would boldly develop platforms in different sectors/regions with true open source being allowed to come into play.

Resistance to the emergence of this fourth scenario may be expected from within the world of officials—politicians and bureaucrats. First, it is not clear that 'open-source federalism' will appeal to provincial and territorial officials who have built their discourse on 'acquired rights' rather than on innovation and experimentation. Second, the pundits in the media (who have systematically attacked decentralization and celebrated state-centricity) have echoed the depth of intellectual programming and the resilience of the mindset that have resulted from sixty years of welfare statism. Third, there is already evidence of some concerted efforts by a fifth-column in the uppermost rank of the federal bureaucracy to suppress and encapsulate all efforts to effect a real reallocation of power toward the provinces and localities, or to open the federal game to experimentation and serious play of the sort upon which open source is built.

Toward a genuine *perestroika*

Organizational culture and the whole philosophy embodied in an institutional order are very difficult to transform. They are quite resistant to change. It is much easier to indulge in some tweaking of the structure and technology to tilt the system out of balance, and thereby trigger more fundamental changes. Moreover, there is no recipe for institutional change, and one can easily understand why Albert Hirschman suggests that when dealing with change, citizens should "modestly respect its unpredictability", for "change can only happen as a result of surprise, otherwise it could not occur at all, for it would be suppressed by the forces that are in favour of the status quo" (Hirschman 1995: 136).

So it is with some circumspection that that we suggest a set of prerequisites and the sort of virtuous scheming necessary if a *perestroika* is to materialize in Canada.

Prerequisites
These prerequisites have to do with getting rid of the mental prisons, inherited from the past, that underpin the present over-centralized institutional order. These constraints are not necessarily well understood, but they are deeply anchored in the Canadian soul. So it is perilous to challenge them, and very difficult to uproot them.

Smoothing the Westminster system

The maxims of Westminster-style government are simple: the separation of the bureaucracy in status from elected politicians; the final authority of ministers in office over the actions of officials; and the lines of accountability running directly from officials to ministers to Cabinet to Parliament. The Canadian federation is a non-interlocking set of a dozen such systems—one for each of the two senior orders of government.

While this is an arcane subject, and most citizens would be unable to define the intricacies of the Westminster system, it has remained a robust feature in the mindset of politicians and bureaucrats alike, and a constant reference point. In a world in which boundaries are blurred, roles are becoming fuzzier, and greater collaboration is called for, these maxims cannot be sustained, and yet, as the Gomery reports show, tradition trumps rationality on this front.

New forms of cooperation between politicians and bureaucrats (who have complementary legitimacies), but also between sectors and levels of government, have *de facto* evolved over time, and new ones will have to materialize. Moreover, it is unthinkable to continue to ignore the centrality of the dozen or so major cities in the country that are the true source of the wealth of the nation, and to treat them as mere 'creatures' of the provinces.

Constitutional amendments may not be a workable route to effect such changes. It is more likely that innovative administrative arrangements will be the most useful instruments. But these innovations will require both a new spirit of collaboration (with an end to parties taking refuge in constitutional wrangles to avoid accepting reasonable administrative arrangements) and the acceptance of soft, intelligent accountability in lieu of the rigid accountability framework implied by the Westminster regime.

Already over the last fifteen years, efficiency considerations have led many federations to try to overcome fragmented competencies, and problems of revenue distribution in the face of vertical fiscal imbalance by modest and tentative initiatives like the Agreement on Internal Trade in

1994, the Canada Health and Social Transfer in 1996, or the Social Union Framework Agreement in 1999 in Canada. But much more limited progress has been made in the development of collaboration at the strategic level. And when it has materialized, it has been through indirect means and in timid ways. The lack of such strategic capacities is a serious disadvantage in a fast changing world (Braun 2008). It is often through strategic selected inattention and much work under the radar screen that progress has been accomplished.

Softening the egalitarian ideology
The second pillar of the old order is the egalitarian ideology that is so often used to bolster the requirement of hyper-centralization. It is argued that decentralization is unworkable because one could not proceed with the required redistribution without the possibility of bringing a sufficient amount of the fiscal resources to the centre. While there has been a slow and painfully-resistant shift from strong to weak egalitarianism over the last few decades, egalitarianism remains a powerful ideology that has prevented efforts to decentralize. There is a need for a decisive attack on this front, and for a change in the language in good currency.

There is something hypocritical about the whole Canadian discourse about egalitarianism. *De facto*, egalitarianism does not guide policy in crucial areas like health and education but only pretends to do so. There seems to be a certain intellectual comfort on the part of both governments and citizens that leads them to collude in wallowing in such rhetorical claims while accepting a significant level of inequality in reality.

One would need to replace the reference to egalitarianism (a most confusing term, that has come to connote a notional and hypothetical entitlement to equality of outcomes) by the more accurate, honest and practical word *equability*—a term that *Merriam-Webster* defines as "lack of noticeable, unpleasant, or extreme variation or inequality". This word provides a more useful reference point in finding the right balance in the practical search for openness, inclusiveness and high-performance, and the inescapable reality of differences. Equability does not entail uniformity.

Sanitizing the human rights language

Human rights discourse is the new despotism. Do-gooders have been so intent on limiting the damage that the tyranny of a majority may inflict on minorities that they have come to defend the tyranny of minorities lyrically, and have fallen into an idolatry of rights as if they were totems. As Michael Ignatieff rightly underlines, "We need to stop thinking of human rights as trumps and begin thinking of them as a language that creates a basis for deliberation" (Ignatieff 2001: 95).

Rights are not a set of trump cards to bring political disputes to closure. Parliament is the place of last resort for deliberation about all governance issues in a democracy. The idea that Parliament is not to be trusted, and that judges as super-bureaucrats are like shamen who cannot be contested, is anti-democratic. The Charter of Rights is a creature of Parliament. Rights have been defined by Parliament. As Ignatieff says, they are a "tool kit against oppression" and one should not automatically "define anything desirable as a right", because that would then erode the legitimacy of core rights (Ibid., 57, 90).

Moreover, courts are not infallible in interpreting the Charter. There is nothing sinister, in a free and democratic society, in Parliament's use of the notwithstanding clause to suspend for a time the application of a decision by the courts that does not pertain to oppression, and with which the majority of freely elected parliamentarians does not agree. To allow minority groups to obtain everything they would 'prefer' when they dress it in a garb of rights, to make rights into a secular religion, and the courts into its only authorized clergy is the gospel in good currency in certain circles.

To reverse this trend will not be easy. Yet the denunciation of the abuse of the rights language and of the indefensible behavior of human rights commissions and other super-bureaucrats has done much over the last while to raise questions about the legitimacy of such claims and the wisdom of the apparatus created to adjudicate them (Leishman 2006; Paquet 2008; Levant 2009). This might ease the transition to a more balanced regime.

Scheming virtuously

Having challenged the canonical references mentioned above, how can one renew Canadian federalism by filling the gaps where there are weak or non-existent mechanisms or unduly loose ligatures? Are practitioners well equipped to do this work? Can one overcome the degree of disinformation and hypocrisy at play? Can one engineer genuine platforms enabling the citizenry to truly become producer of governance?

For the sort of tinkering that we suggest to be useful, three conditions are necessary: there is a need for practitioners to act locally and 'at the mechanisms level' but also (i) to develop a super-vision, to maintain a broad holistic perspective, and to keep the theory and its professionals, the experience of the practitioners, and the interests of all the stakeholders in the given area somewhat aligned; (ii) to ensure the highest and best use of the technologies of collaboration, of self-organization, and of positive deviance by those who have a capacity to confront and to be critical of the ways in good currency; and (iii) to set various platforms for experimentation in the different issue domains.

Super-vision

The main objectives are to avoid the tyranny of small decisions, to escape from the tyranny of disciplines and ideologies that provide truncated and reductive images of reality, and to take into account the centrality of key complementarities and the power of context (Gladwell 2000; Surowiecki 2004). This is necessary in order to avoid doing more damage than good. But there are very serious barriers to such work that lie in the traditional approaches to social architecture even when the challenges are faced with the best of intentions. There is often misalignment among individual practitioners' skills, issue domains, professional fields, and other stakeholders' interests. Indeed, according to Gardner et al. (2001), creativity and good work by professionals are the result of a good alignment of these four realities.

Practitioners of public social architecture have a certain specific knowledge and skill set that they have developed through learning by doing—their Delta knowledge (Gilles and Paquet 1989). They maintain somewhat opposed tendencies: a good deal of curiosity and an open mind, but also a quasi-obsessive commitment and perseverance.

Moreover, they operate in a symbolic system: the world of public policy (which, like the world of medicine, journalism, carpentry, etc. is built on two sets of codes: a set of procedural ideas (equipment, purposes, identities) and a set of ethical standards (assurance that those ideas will not be used against the common interest) (Spinosa, Flores and Dreyfus 1997).

But at the same time, these and other professionals are more than skilled persons operating in a domain; they also exercise their profession in a field, i.e., a social network of practitioners, a tribe that has its mores, habits, standards, priorities and taboos. As such, they are not only guided by the imperatives of skills and tasks, but also by the values of the tribe.

Finally, the practitioners/professionals, domains and fields all operate in a broader world that involves a wide array of other stakeholders (the corporate world, the general public, etc.) who hold very different views of the world and with whom practitioners and professionals must interact in productive ways.

It should be clear that the super-vision one is striving for must be made to emerge bottom-up through joint work on aligning individual practitioners' skills, issue domains, professional fields, and other stakeholders' interests. The state will be only one of the stakeholders involved in this sort of work. Open sourcing entails allowing as many of those with a serious interest to partake in the genesis of the most effective alignment.

There may be efforts by the central state apparatus to impose a super-vision in the name of convenience or operational simplicity. Much of the virtuous scheming required may at times be dedicated to ensuring that such efforts to impose unsuitable arrangements are appropriately stunted.

It may be naive to expect that all the components will ever be perfectly in sync (the baskets of skills and interests of practitioners/professionals, the definition of the issue domains, the values of the tribe and the interests of other stakeholders) since they are all in flux. But one may expect that they will tend to converge toward some evolving configuration that will tend to accommodate somewhat all these constraints simultaneously.

If the alignment is imperfect, practitioners/professionals and stakeholders (of which the state is not an unimportant one) will be led, in the name of efficiency, effectiveness, resilience and innovation to use new or adjusted skills for new or adjusted tasks in the issue domains in which they operate, to view the value of their profession in a whole new context, and to learn to interact with other stakeholders in new and different ways.

The issue domain itself will thereby evolve to match the 'real issues', the fields will tend to be reconfigured so that the investigation is not unduly restricted by crippling paradigms, and the debating forums and platforms will evolve to accommodate and bring together the various old and new stakeholders, each of whom may harbour quite different values and priorities. Such inter-adjustments may take time but they will evolve as the system thrives to extricate itself from its many conflictive equilibria.

Connexity, self-organization and the failure to confront

A great deal of work is needed to reframe issue domains in a more realistic and wholesome way, to reconfigure the disciplinary fields, to generate more dialogue and deliberation with other stakeholders in order to elicit collaborative governance. Would-be social architects and engineers as "reflective practitioners" will require new skills (Schön 1983) and it is not sure that one can count on the adjustment process unfolding necessarily smoothly and quickly.

Three impediments to smooth adjustment are the dismal neglect of what the new information technologies are making possible for democracy; the obscurantist denial of the forces of self-organization; and the failure to confront that allows so many untruths to remain in good currency.

(i) It is not the place to celebrate information technologies but it is crucial to notice that new bottom-up tools exist that enable mass collaboration, broad-based engagement and deliberation (Mulgan 1997; Lenihan et al. 2007; Tapscott and Williams 2006). These tools are not used half as much as they should be. As a result, even though governments and agencies have access to the sort of machinery to make use of the intelligence spread throughout society, share information more readily, and assess the link between policy and outcome more rigorously, the command-and-control military model of those who claim the right to speak in the name of all remains the archetype in good currency.

These new technologies of cooperation are going to play an essential role in demonstrating, via pilot projects, the possibility of generating new opportunities for complex cooperative strategies that change the way people work together to solve problems, generate wealth and contribute to governance (Saveri et al. 2005, 2008). The new technologies allow organizations to push power to the edge: it is a matter in which both business and military organizations are already familiar, but there has been much resistance in the public governance world to allowing the equivalent of a Green Beret master sergeant on a satellite phone calling up a B-2 bomber to drop ordnances on a specific point (Lawlor 2006). This is a matter calling for a revolution in the mind.

(ii) An equally important change in mindset is required in the appreciation of self-organization. One of the most important blockages in the development of effective coordination when power, resources and information are widely distributed is (1) the strong reluctance of rational actors to accept the seemingly incomprehensible (and quasi-magical, in their view) emergence of some order from seemingly chaotic environments, and (2) the strong propensity to make use of episodic monumental failures of this process as persuasive, determining evidence that one cannot ever rely on

self-organization and self-steering and that one must ensure
that some one is in charge always and robustly so.

This is not the place to develop a full counter-argument to
this skeptical stance, but one cannot ask the reader to accept
a paper arguing that this is the most promising way out of
the present quandary without at least providing a sketchy
plausible counter-argument.

This counter-argument builds first on a better understanding of the way in which collaboration materializes in
large groups. Collaboration is first and foremost dependent upon communication generating social negotiation
and creative output. Such mass collaboration was first
observed and studied in animal societies, where it has been
shown that explicit and conscious social negotiation was
not necessary for mass collaboration to materialize. It is in
this context that Pierre-Paul Grasse has coined the term
"stigmergy" to connote a method of communication (and
implicit negotiation) in which individuals communicate
with one another by modifying their local environment.
It helps us understand "how disparate, distributed, *ad hoc*
contributions could lead to the emergence of the largest
collaborative enterprises" (Elliott 2006).

A new literacy about self-organization is needed to
understand and make sense of collaboration. Its origin is
in the emergence of social dilemmas in which individual
rationality would appear to lead to collective irrationality.
The best example is the tragedy of the commons, where
common property resources are depleted by the overuse of
the resource as a result of each myopic individual trying to
make the highest and best use of it for himself. A relatively
simple and yet powerful avenue out of this sort of dilemma
is the development of a broader perspective through generating common knowledge: partaking in rituals producing common knowledge, i.e., letting all know exactly what
other audience members know. Once, other persons' views
are made known, collaboration is made possible. Indeed,
increasing common knowledge becomes a way to foster
coordination and collaboration (Chwe 2001).

In all such self-organizing worlds, there always are some
critical thresholds at which, after gradual change that left

the system unmoved, an additional minute change sets the system adrift in search of a new equilibrium. The whole management literature on tipping points is based on the recognition that a better understanding of the cognitive and organizational space reveals where the system might afford the possibility of effective intervention (Shapiro 2003).

The complexity of such adjustments poses wicked problems to potential interveners. On the one hand, unintended consequences, network externalities and cumulative causation at critical points—part of the dynamics of self-organization—often swamp the original intervention and neutralize or distort its impact; on the other hand, these forces may, if one has a fair strategic understanding of the dynamics of self-organization, amplify and enrich the impact of an anonymous intervention in an open-source context.

(iii) A third necessary change in the mindset has to do with the failure to confront.

"Conflict is central to the intellectual mode of intellectual life, criticism. Criticism involves the formation of a judgment towards something that the critic believes could—and typically should—have been otherwise" (Fuller 2005: 149). Democracy feeds on robust debates; but such debates often entail great personal cost when political correctness becomes *"un nouveau et indolore despotisme"* (Delsol 2005).

Despite strong impressions to the contrary, such tensions and conflicts are the fount of social cohesion. This Gauchet-Dubiel thesis, elegantly defended by Albert Hirschman (1995: 235ff), suggests that a society with freedom of speech and association that produces "a steady diet of conflicts that need to be addressed and that the society learns to manage" acquires vitality, and a capacity to renew itself. It underlines the important role of the intellectual as conflict-generator, and as the indirect source of social cohesion through the conflicts he/she stimulates.

Failure to confront can afflict individuals as well as governments (and other organizations). Both can be profoundly destructive.

It is always unpleasant (except for sadists) to confront a person whose performance is unsatisfactory and to demand that some corrective measures be taken. It is probably the most important weakness of stewards in all sorts of organizations: the lack of capability or willingness to look a person directly reporting to one in the eye, and to say that "this will not do". Yet, failure to confront is tantamount to deception, to not telling the truth, to misinforming. The chronic unwillingness to confront may arise from fear of challenges, rejection by others, tribal 'shunning' or disapproval, from being ridiculed, or fear of an interaction one cannot control, or simply as a result of a lack of self-confidence and courage.

Failure to confront entails some reprehensible disengagement, some unacceptable strategic silence in the face of situations calling for correctives. It may also condone and nurture some 'learned helplessness'—a reaction of passivity in the face of unpleasant, harmful or damaging situations where one senses that one has neither bargaining power nor capacity to resolve the problem.

While there has been a good deal of theatrics and antics by politicians (and much disinformation generated in the process), genuine confrontation has been regarded by the citizenry as distasteful and much has been allowed to survive because of the great deference to authority in Canada, and a quasi-veneration for consensus that has degenerated into some sort of 'collegiality' disease that is the obverse of the sort of robust and frank multilogue that is of foundational importance in collaboration and cooperation.

For open source federalism to have any chance of thriving, critical thinking must be reinstated as a dominant value in lieu of the prevalent conformism. Cleansing the communication systems of 'scorias' (crippling epistemologies, ideological filtres, cognitive dissonance, political correctness and the like, that prevent the information and communication system from functioning well, and that therefore generate institutional and organizational pathologies, and governance failures) must become the new imperative.

The central importance of critical thinking and confrontation amounts to nothing less than an invitation to subversion (Paquet 2009a, b).

Sectional/regional platforms

A promising way to develop the least inadequate organizational form is not to impose it cold on an assemblage of interested parties, but to allow it to emerge once the nature of relevant prototypes is ascertained on the basis of what the stakeholders will come to regard as non-negotiable constraints. The key to this evolution on the basis of prototypes is:

- a drift toward open source governance (i.e., a form of governance that enables each meaningful partner as much as possible to have access to the "code", and to "tinker" freely with the way the system works within certain well-accepted constraints) (Sabel 2001); and
- a priority given to "serious play" (i.e., a premium on experimentation with the imperfect prototypes that might be improved by retooling, restructuring and reframing in productive and innovative ways (Schrage 2000).

What will be required are sectional/regional platforms corresponding to the overall terrain of issues domains and communities of meaning or communities of fate (i.e., assemblages of people united in their common concern for shared problems, or a shared passion for a topic or set of issues). It is tantamount to identifying a vast number of sub-games that each requires a specific approach. Each issue-domain (health, education, environment, etc.—or maybe some sub-issue domain like mental health) is multifaceted, and dealt with on an *ad hoc* basis with the view of allowing the design of its own stewardship to emerge.

This open system approach takes into account the people with a substantial stake in the issue domain, the resources available and the culture in place, and allows experiments to shape the required mix of principles and norms, and rules and decision-making procedures likely to promote the preferred mix of efficiency, resilience and learning. A template likely to be of use across the board may not be available yet, but that does not mean that a workable one cannot be elicited *hic et nunc* (Sabel 2004).

However, it is not sufficient to ensure open access, one must also ensure that the appropriate motivations are nurtured so that all those who have a substantial stake are willing and able to engage in 'serious play' (i.e., become truly producers of governance through tinkering with the governance apparatus within certain limits).

Taking communities of meaning seriously suggests not only that very different arrangements are likely to emerge from place to place, but underlines the importance of regarding any such arrangement as essentially temporary: the ground is in motion, and diversity is likely to acquire new faces, so different patterns of organizational designs are likely to emerge.

Consequently, governance would not only rely on a much more flexible toolbox, but would require that any formal or binding arrangement be revisited, played with, and adjusted to take into account the evolving diversity of circumstances. It would open the door to the design of more complex and innovative arrangements, likely to deal more effectively with deep diversity.

Prototyping would appear to be the main activity underpinning serious play:

- identifying some top requirements as quickly as possible;
- putting in place a provisional medium of co-development;
- allowing as many interested parties as possible to get involved as partners in improving the arrangement;
- encouraging iterative prototyping; and
- thereby encouraging all, through playing with prototypes, to get a better understanding of the problems, of their priorities and of themselves (Schrage 2000: 199ff).

The purpose of the exercise is to create a dialogue (creative interaction) between people and prototypes. This may be more important than creating a dialogue between people. It is predicated on a culture of active participation that would need to be nurtured.

The sort of democratization of design that ensues and the sort of playfulness that is required for 'serious play' with prototypes, are essential for the process to succeed, and they apply equally well to narrow or broad organizational concerns.

The most promising of these platforms for experimentation would be city-regions. The argument has been made quite forcefully that existing large mega-cities like Toronto, Montreal and Vancouver have been crippled by the strictures imposed on their governance by the provincial (and at times the federal) authorities. City-regions are a main source of the wealth of the country and face challenges quite different from the provinces they are nested in: they are more diverse, and as a result require services that are quite different from rural areas. Not only have they been denied access to the whole range of taxes and revenue streams, they have often been prevented from using their margins of maneuverability by provincial vetoes.

Since the city-regions represent communities of meaning and communities of purpose, and since they are territorially well defined, they would appear to represent particularly convenient platforms for experimentation (Broadbent 2008).

Conclusion

Innovative 'bricolage' entails almost necessarily some trespassing and some conversations across boundaries. Innovation is a social process and the more successful the innovation, the more social the process. Lester and Piore (2004) describe the early stages of innovation as a cocktail party where diverse people gather and chat, casually but seriously, about a variety of topics, in a safe and stimulating environment.

If one had to put a finger on the major failure of the Canadian institutional order, it might be the lack of such forums. Our overly rigid governing regime does not allow for (or at least robustly constrains) the free-form exchange of ideas, and this rigidity (together with the lack of forums) often condemns organizations to a future of 'unimaginative product extensions' when what is needed is reframing. Emerson's light bulb was not discovered on a journey to improve the candle. Tinkering with information flows, creating new forums, and stimulating new partnerships may appear innocuous, but the sort of trespassing, 'bricolage' and *métissage* likely to ensue may hold the key to such reframing.

It would not be prudent to predict a thawing of the Canadian ethos that will proceed in a revolutionary way, or advance quickly. There may be a *perestroika* in the making, but it will proceed in a hesitant, meandering, two-steps-forward-and-one-step-back and/or oblique kind of fashion. This is the Canadian way.

The broad changes in the texture of the socio-economy brought about by globalization and accelerated technical change have revealed the limits of the nation-state in managing complex problems. Not only has governing become less state-centric, but also the very notion of the public sector itself has been transformed: it has become a multi-level, multi-polar, network-like de-centred reality subject to a new "relational rationality" (Ladeur 2004).

In this sense, the hard core of the 'technocratic state' is becoming eroded not only by the growing intrusion of politics but also by the proliferation of loose regimes that take different forms depending on the issue domain and may not include the public sector as a major player.

Such regimes are the new fabric of the Canadian federation—based on networks that not only go beyond the scope of the state, but also do not follow traditional models of organizational design because they are shaped by the expectations and constraints of a variety of actors (mostly non-public sector), often with different perspectives and different contributions to make.

In effect:

> ...(t)he (S)tate can no longer deliver stable rules of guid-
> ance for private actors ... but it has to fine-tune limited
> interventions in the process of private management...In
> this sense, the possibilities generated from private action
> create a domain of options which is, at the same time,
> the pre-structure on which public regulation has to draw
> (Ladeur 2004: 17).

Open-source experimentation at the regimes and issue
domains level will create an entirely new dynamic in Canadian federalism. It will allow citizens and emergent publics
to become producers of governance, and push the decentralization process one major step forward. While the aim is
to re-empower the citizenry, it cannot and will not be done
across the board in one sweep: it will have to be built on
issue domain experiments and regime building.

Canadians are ready for such experimentation, but,
before confederal governance can take hold of them, the citizenry of Canada must build the requisite "negative capacity" (as Keats would call it)—that is, the capacity to keep
going when things are going wrong. This entails the construction of the necessary support systems not only to help
the citizens to take creative part in this multilogue, but also
to withstand the chilling effect generated by the setbacks
that will accompany any change venture of this sort. Para-
doxically, this will require support from the strategic state
and therefore a revolution in the mind first.

Whether the new strategic state is likely to favour such
experimentation will gradually emerge, or whether the
right to take part and experiment will have to be wrestled
from reluctant state powers remains to be seen. But what
is certain is that the contours of the new emerging system
are beginning to be perceptible—something that Innerarity
calls "social liberalism", a system that has clearly a Proud-
honesque flavor (Innerarity 2006: 235; Proudhon 1850).

Federal systems like Canada that have already slaughtered the sacred cow of whole and indivisible sovereignty
will probably be in the *avant-garde* of this movement even if,

like Canada, they are likely to proceed slowly and cautiously. 'Social liberalism' with its emphasis of cooperative freedom is a natural extension of the logic of federalism. Proudhon has been wrongly caricatured as a utopian socialist. In fact, freedom was the fundamental tenet of his social philosophy. His objective was to fight "*la paresse des masses*" (the inertia of the citizenry) which is at the origin of authoritarianism, and "*le préjugé gouvernmental*" (the propensity to rely too much and automatically on the state) instead of having enough confidence that the citizenry can indeed be a producer of governance. This is the very spirit of our proposals.

References

Agamben, Giorgio 2003. *État d'exception*. Paris: Seuil.

Ashby, W. Ross 1956. *Introduction to Cybernetics*. London: Chapman & Hall.

Benkler, Yochai 2006. *The Wealth of Networks*. New Haven: Yale University Press.

Boisot, Max 1995. *Information Space*. London: Routledge.

Braun, Dietmar 2008. "Making Federalism More Efficient: A Comparative Assessment." *Acta Politica*, 43: 1: 4–25.

Broadbent, Alan 2008. *Urban Nation*. Toronto: HarperCollins.

Burelle, André 2005. *Pierre Elliott Trudeau*. Montreal: Fides.

Carter, Stephen L. 1998. *The Dissent of the Governed*. Cambridge, MA: Harvard University Press.

Chwe, M. S. W. 2001. *Rational Ritual*. Princeton: Princeton University Press.

Delsol, Chantal 2005 (January-March). "Le Nouveau despotisme." *Géopolitique*, 89: 25.

Dror, Yehezkel 1997. "Delta-type Senior Civil Service for the 21st Century." *International Review of Administrative Sciences*, 63: 1: 7–23.

Elliott, Mark 2006. "Stigmergic Collaboration: The Evolution of Group Work." *M/C Journal* 9: 2 http://journal.media-culture.org.au/0605/03-elliott.php. [consulted August 8, 2008].

Fuller, L. Lon 2001. *The Principles of Social Order*. Portland, Oregon: Hart Publishing.

Fuller, Steve 2005. *The Intellectual*. Cambridge, UK: iconbooks.

Garud, Raghu, et al. eds. 2003. *Managing in the Modular Age*. Oxford: Blackwell.

Gardner, Howard et al. 2001. *Good Work*. New York: Basic Books.

Gilles, Willem, and Gilles Paquet 1989. "On Delta Knowledge." In *Edging toward Year 2000*, eds. G. Paquet and M. von Zur Muehlen. Ottawa: Canadian Federation of Deans of Management and Administrative Studies, 15–30.

Gintis, Herbert et al. eds. 2005. *Moral Sentiments and Material Interest*. Cambridge, MA: The MIT Press.

Gladwell, Malcolm 2000. *The Tipping Point*. Boston: Little Brown & Company.

Goldsmith, Stephen, William D. Eggers 2004. *Governing by Networks*. Washington: Brookings Institution Press.

Hirschman, Albert O. 1995. *A Propensity to Self-Subversion*. Cambridge, MA: Harvard University Press.

Holland, John H. 1995. *Hidden Order*. Reading, MA: Addison-Wesley.

Hubbard, Ruth and Gilles Paquet 2007. *Gomery`s Blinders and Canadian Federalism*. Ottawa: The University of Ottawa Press.

Ignatieff, Michael 2001. *Human Rights as Politics and Idolatry*. Princeton, NJ: Princeton University Press.

Innerarity, Daniel 2006. *La démocratie sans l'État–Essai sur la gouvernement des sociétés complexes*. Paris: Climats.

Jacobs, Jane 1992. *Systems of Survival*. New York: Vintage Books.

Ladeur, Karl-Heinz 2004. *Public Governance in the Age of Globalization*. Aldershot: Ashgate.

Lawlor, Maryann 2006 (May). "Collaborative Technologies Demand Deep Change." *SIGNAL Magazine*.

Le Grand, Julian 2003. *Motivation, Agency and Public Policy*. Oxford: Oxford University Press.

Leishman, Rory 2006. *Against Judicial Activism*. Toronto: The University of Toronto Press.

Lenihan, Donald et al. 2007. *Progressive Governance for Canadians*. Ottawa: Crossing Boundaries.

Lester, Richard K. and Michael J. Piore 2004. *Innovation: The Missing Dimension*. Cambridge, MA: Harvard University Press.

Levant, Ezra 2009. *Shakedown*. Toronto: McClelland & Stewart.

Mulgan, Geoff. 1997. *Connexity*. Boston, MA: Harvard Business School Press.

Naisbitt, John 1994. *Global Paradox*. New York: William Morrow.

O'Neill, Onora 2002. *A Question of Trust*. Cambridge, UK: Cambridge University Press.

O'Toole, James 1995. *Leading Change*. San Francisco: Jossey-Bass.

Paquet, Gilles 1977. "Federalism as Social Technology." In *Options. Conference on the Future of the Canadian Federation*, ed. J. Evans. Toronto: The University of Toronto Press, 281–302.

Paquet, Gilles 1996–97. "The Strategic State." *Ciencia Ergo Sum*, 3: 3: 1996: 257–261 (Part 1); 4: 1: 1997: 28–34 (Part 2); 4: 2: 1997: 148–154 (Part 3).

Paquet, Gilles 1997. "Alternative Program Delivery: Transforming the Practices of Governance." In *Alternative Service Delivery: Sharing Governance in Canada*, eds. R. Ford and D. R. Zussman. Toronto: IPAC/ KPMG, 31–58.

Paquet, Gilles 1999. "Innovations in Governance in Canada." *Optimum*, 29: 2–3: 71–81.

Paquet, Gilles 2001 (Winter). "P3 Governance: A Power Game without a Master." *Summit: The Business of Public Sector Procurement*, 6–7.

Paquet, Gilles 2004. "Gouvernance et déconcertation." *Optimumonline*, 34 : 4 : 18–46.

Paquet, Gilles 2005. *The New Geo-Governance: A Baroque Approach*. Ottawa: The University of Ottawa Press.

Paquet, Gilles 2008. *Deep Cultural Diversity*. Ottawa: The University of Ottawa Press.

Paquet, Gilles 2009a. *Crippling Epistemologies and Governance Failures*. Ottawa: The University of Ottawa Press.

Paquet, Gilles 2009b. *Scheming Virtuously: The Road to Collaborative Governance*. Ottawa: Invenire Books.

Parker, Simon and Niamh Gallagher 2007. *The Collaborative State*. London: Demos.

Proudhon, Pierre-Joseph 1850. *Confessions d'un révolutionnaire*. Paris: Garnier Frères.

Sabel, Charles F. 2001. "A Quiet Revolution of Democratic Governance: Towards Democratic Experimentalism." In *Governance in the 21st Century*. Paris: OECD, 121–148.

Sabel, Charles F. 2004. "Beyond Principal-Agent Governance: Experimnentalist Organizations, Learning and Accountability." In *De Staat van de Democratie. Democratie Voorbij de Staat*, eds. E. Engelen and M. Sie Dhian Ho. Amsterdam: Amsterdam University Press, 173–195.

Sacconi, Lorenzo 2000. *The New Social Contract*. Heidelberg: Springer.

Saveri, Andrea et al. 2005. *Technologies of Cooperation*. Palo Alto: Institute for the Future.

Saveri, Andrea et al. 2008 (Summer). "Technologies of Cooperation: A Socio-Technical Framework for Robust 4G." *Technology and Society Magazine* IEEE, 11–23.

Schön, Donald A. 1971. *Beyond the Stable State*. New York: Norton.

Schön, Donald A. 1983. *The Reflective Practitioner*. New York: Basic Books

Schrage, Michael 2000. *Serious Play*. Boston, MA: Harvard Business School Press.

Shapiro, Andrea 2003. *Creating Contagious Commitment—Applying the Tipping Point to Organizational Change.* Hillsborough, NC: Strategy Perspective.

Shirky, Clay 2008. *Here Comes Everybody.* New York: The Penguin Press.

Spinosa, Charles et al. 1997. *Disclosing New Worlds.* Cambridge, MA: The MIT Press.

Stein, Janice G. 2006. "Canada by Mondrian: Networked Federalism in an Era of Globalization." In *Canada by Picasso—The Faces of Federalism,* eds. R. Gibbins et al. Ottawa: The Conference Board of Canada, 15–58.

Sunstein, Cass R. 2006. *Infotopia.* Oxford: Oxford University Press.

Surowiecki, James 2004. *The Wisdom of Crowds.* New York: Doubleday.

Tapscott, Don and Anthony D. Williams 2006. *Wikinomics.* New York: Portfolio.

Taylor, Carl 1997. "The ACIDD Test: A Framework for Policy Planning and Decision-Making." *Optimum,* 27: 4: 53–62.

Thuderoz, Christian et al. 1999. *La confiance.* Paris: Gaëtan Morin.

Wenger, Etienne et al. 2002. *Cultivating Communities of Practice.* Boston, MA: Harvard Business School Press.

Yankelovich, Daniel and Steven Rosell 2000. www.viewpointlearning.org [accessed April 16, 2010].

Decentralized Federalism as Baroque Experiment

Ruth Hubbard and Gilles Paquet

> *...the key to explaining human development*
> *is the transition from a social order that limits access*
> *to political and economic participation*
> *to one that encourages open access.*
>
> —D. C. North

Decentralization is consubstantial with federalism. Building on principles of subsidiarity, a federal culture of shared sovereignty, and an empowerment of the citizenry would appear to be not only workable, but desirable, and the way of the future in a world of ever greater diversity. But such an apparatus must be conceived around new units of analysis: sustainable regimes within a legitimate if loosely integrated order.

Stephen Krasner has defined regimes as "sets of implicit and explicit principles, norms, rules and decision-making procedures around which actors' expectations converge in a given area of international relations" (Krasner 1993: 2). This definition has been refined and expanded by Hasenclever et al., who have made the different conceptual elements of the definition more explicit:

> ...principles are beliefs of fact, causation and rectitude. Norms are standards of behavior defined in terms of rights and obligation. Rules are specific prescriptions or proscriptions for action. Decision-making procedures are

prevailing practices for making and implementing collective choice (Hasenclever et al.1997: 9).

Regimes, wherever they may be, are arrangements
designed to ensure effective and robust coordination when
power, information and resources are widely distributed.
Different regime theories have emphasized one aspect or
another of this challenge. For instance, some have insisted
mainly on the 'power' variable, and made the other dimensions more or less dependent on the outcome of the power
struggle. Others have emphasized the resources base of
the interest groups in competition, and used the language
of 'interdependency' of game theorists to emphasize the
dominant role of patterns of resources and situational variables in shaping the outcome. Another group has focused
on information and knowledge as the key dimensions, and
posited learning as the core force at work in 'epistemic communities'.

There is no reason to believe that these views are mutually exclusive.

All these forces are at work in shaping the sort of regimes
that are likely to be effective, robust and capable of generating social learning. Consequently, regimes are likely to be
hybrid forms of organization that will accommodate these
three sources of tensions.

Foundations of regimes and ecologies of governance

The foundational elements of a regime have been described
in various ways. They are of necessity only loosely definable,
since they have to adjust to the particular circumstances of
each issue domain, and to the configuration of interests and
communities at play.

The terrain on which regimes grow can be mapped simply in a three-dimensional box, spelling out the major families of forces at work (power, interdependency, cognition),
the two sources of order (principles and norms, and rules

and decision-making procedures), and the three main objectives pursued (efficiency, robustness, and resilience/learning). See figure 7.1.

Regimes are, in effect, arrangements attempting to deal with divergent problem—problems that, as they get clarified, reveal fundamental differences in viewpoints. Such problems can only generate loose moral contracts around which actor expectations converge only to some degree. They are neither orderly nor systematic, but reveal some internal consistency and technical proficiency. Regimes cannot be of general application: they are identified in terms of problem areas, and define the framework that prevails in the coordination function in a particular area or domain. For instance, while a country may espouse the globalization syndrome in matters of trade, it may remain mercantilist when it comes to human capital and outright exclusionist when it comes to culture and social integration, even though these approaches may not be perceived as universally desirable.

To the extent that the *terrain des operations* is quite diverse, and the array of interested stakeholders also quite varied,

Figure 7.1   The regime space

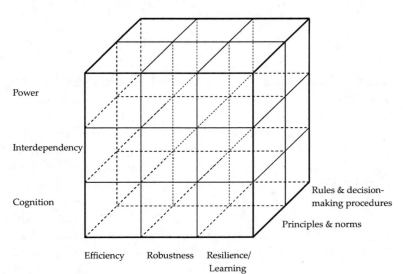

the best way to accommodate such terrains and such stake-holders is often by dealing with them 'relatively separately'. In the same way that internationally regimes are defined pertaining to special terrains (fisheries, environment, etc.), we would suggest that the same imperative applies on the national scene, in the face of deep diversity and turbulent times and on the basis of local 'super-visions'.

By partitioning the terrain into issue domains and 'com-munities of meaning', it is possible to identify a vast number of sub-games that require specific treatment. This partition-ing does not exclude some attention being given to territory and nation, but it does not provide these dimensions with the dominant role. Each issue domain is multifaceted, and dealt with on an *ad hoc* basis.

The expression "ecology of governance" has been pro-posed by Walt Anderson to identify this new fluid form of governance: "many different systems and different kinds of systems interacting with one another, like the multiple organisms in an ecosystem" (Anderson 2001: 252). Such arrangements are not necessarily "neat, peaceful, stable or efficient ... but in a continual process of learning and chang-ing and responding to feedback". This represents a trans-versal nexus of arrangements within the regime space.

An ecology of governance amounts to a group of loosely integrated 'uncentralized networks', designed around issue domains. A regime-based federalism would be one designed to facilitate social learning by ensuring that such networks correspond roughly to both issue domains and 'communi-ties of meaning', while taking into account territorial and national dimensions often only as constraints (Kohr 1978).

Such ecology of governance must remain an open system that has the capacity to learn and to evolve: the model is not a cathedral but a bazaar (Raymond 2001). The opera-tions of this open system in turn shape the required mix of principles and norms, but also of rules and decision-making procedures likely to promote the preferred mix of efficiency, resilience and learning in the different issue domains.

Issue domains are not to be simply allotted to 'territo-ries' or 'nations' but are the locus of an arena where the different interested communities (including territorial and national officials) would partake in the design of a participative organizational form, allowing the appropriate mix of collaboration and competition in the spirit of cooperative freedom. One would, for instance, deal with the issue of health (or even with the sub-issue 'mental health') within an appropriate forum, in the same way that forums are created internationally to handle critical issues, and accords or agreements of all sorts are arrived at in such forums.

Such efforts to fit the forum to the issue may appear unwieldy if pushed beyond certain limits, but there are advantages to disunion (Kohr 1941). It opens organizational design to all sorts of new mixes to accommodate the variegated nature of the fabric of socio-technical systems in an improved way. In some cases, devolution might entail delegation to local communities that are likely to better fit both territorial and social imperatives. In other cases, however, one may have to sacrifice some territorial expediency to satisfy the demands of variegated communities.

No general template is available yet (and indeed it may not exist) that is likely to apply mechanically across the board in a regime-based federalism, but experiments in the private sector have shown that uncentralized networks are workable arrangements, even in complex transnational settings. The most interesting practical application is the "chaord": the model used for the organizational design of VISA. If such an organization form, rooted explicitly in the principle of subsidiarity, can coordinate the work of over 23,000 financial institutions operating in over 200 countries and serving over 335 million users in a segment of the world system, and if it can do it effectively, it may well serve as a plausible template or at least as a promising prototype in our search for effective models of federalism (Hock 1995). The same confederal spirit is a reference point in the construction of international arrangements (Paquet 2009).

The fact also that such a scheme has proved effective, efficient and resilient in the private sector and at the transnational level has not only challenged the centralized mindset that is omnipresent in large organizations effectively, but it also suggests that it may well meet the requirement of overall coherence required by the 'strategic state' (Paquet 1996–97).

This approach is likely to give heartburn to traditional analysts of federalism who focus their attention strictly on stylized political and administrative relations, on intra-state intergovernmental conflicts, and primitive public finance concoctions. If they loathe ambiguity (as many do), the pain will be greater. As suggested in many of the chapters in this volume, this mechanical view of federalism and the undue attention given to surface administrative phenomena are bound, in our view, to yield limited insights.

Federalism as collaborative regime

The technologies of collaboration are guideposts, moral contracts, conventions and the like, which are the core of regimes. They define not only the processes through which coordination occurs, but the ways in which (implicitly) the limits beyond which one is not allowed to proceed are defined—very much as the speed limit on the road implicitly spells out what is regarded as the tolerable death toll on our roads. But there is often a large gap between the rules and the state of mind of the population and thus, the 'rules in use'. Rules can be defined in the light of sanctimonious discourses and do not always match real processes. Unintended consequences reveal that what would appear on the surface as reasonable is in reality not workable here and now. Good governance entails a process of guiding which is transparent, inclusive, participative and fairly effective through the crafting of arrangements that are generally in keeping with the dominant logic of the regime, and likely to generate a 'capacity to transform' as circumstances change.

Until now, there has been an attempt to collapse most issues into arenas and agoras defined by territorial/national debates. This is unduly reductive. In a deeply diverse world, where such reduction is necessarily counter-productive, the only way to construct a coherent order is to tailor the arrangements pertaining to issue areas in ways that may not be territorial/national. Instead of trying to allocate all the issues of interest to rigidly defined 'layers' of decision-making authorities, collective decision-making arrangements must be designed around issues, while respecting autonomy, but fostering collaboration in order to suit the circle of stakeholders who have a genuine, significant and knowledgeable interest in the issue.

Instead of territory becoming the 'essence', it remains a convenient conduit on occasion. Nationality can also be a useful conduit but not necessarily a categorical imperative. There may also be other conduits depending on the nature of the issue. For instance, in the case of health, it may turn out that the catchment area is a crucially relevant unit of analysis. This would mean that governing major portions of the health care system on other bases may be very inefficient. In still other cases, personal federalism may be the obvious 'superior' solution: dividing the social system into associations of individuals with certain characteristics. At still other times, one might want to use, as the basis of operation, the *communauté nationale* in the sense proposed by André Laurendeau (Paquet 2000). But as Kohr has shown, there are significant costs to such a basis of operations, and it has been a major source of divergent problems that have too often proved intractable because of their categorical nature.

There is obviously a need for a minimal foundational set of basic principles that would apply to all these arrangements in very much the same manner that basic foundational principles were defined in the case of VISA. There may not be unanimity at this time about what these principles should be, but it is not a utopian quest to work at defining them. They would probably refer (among other things) to maximum participation of all interested stakeholders (to ensure legitimacy), competition (i.e., overlapping jurisdictions), subsidiarity (i.e., genuine decentralization) and multistability (i.e., segmentation into issue domains for the strategies to be more tractable and to immunize against crashes of the whole social system) (Paquet 2008: chapter 5)

This would allow a new reconfiguration of federalism that takes 'communities of meaning' and 'social learning' seriously, and allows their import to weigh heavily in the definition of federalism as social technology. Territory and nation would continue to have some importance, but they would see their import mitigated by the new imperatives of diversity and social learning. Such an approach may suggest very different arrangements, but would underline the importance of regarding any arrangement arrived at as essentially temporary—since the ground is in motion, and diversity is likely to acquire new faces.

Consequently, a regime-based federalism would not only rely on a much more flexible toolbox, but would probably require that any formal or binding arrangement be revisited regularly in the same way as is done with the *Bank Act* or company law.

Ecological rationality

This ensemble of baroque decentralized experiments is bound to be opposed by those guided by a single-valued imperative (be it administrative expediency, egalitarianism, etc.) that trumps all other considerations. For those 'narrow optimizers' or 'solutionnists', rationality is naively defined as maximizing simple-minded objective functions subject to rigid constraints. This sort of skimpy rationality drives strategies that are dominated by some anaemic order of beliefs.

Ecological rationality is not mainly concerned with internal arbitrary criteria, but by the match between strategy and environment. It is not driven by the fiction of optimization in the manner of Dr. Spock in *Star Trek*—obsessively using high-tech logic tools. Such a Spockish approach often tends to mis-characterize the nature of the problem when the environment is complex, turbulent and evolving. Reification is the effete label for this disease.

More balanced human beings put things in context, build on the accumulated experiences of their whole sensory system, and make use not only of their rational logic but also of their social and emotional logics (Polski 2008: 68ff). They take into account the external state of affairs, the internal state of mind, and the brain state: agents "feeling their way" use heuristics (taking all these elements into account) that

combine accuracy with speed and frugality—that are ecologically rational—in making adaptive decisions (Gigerenzer 2002: 47ff)

A strategy is ecologically rational not as result of sole
coherence and internal consistency, but when it is adapted
to its external environment. One cannot expect more from
our organizations. The general conclusion of this volume is
that decentralized federalism is likely to prevail against the
centralized mindset in good currency because it is 'ecologically rational'.

The common thread throughout the book has been the
variety of ways in which decentralization would appear
to ensure, better, that: (1) the differentiated preferences of
deeply diverse societies will be taken seriously, (2) variety
will effectively be produced, and (3) the innovation and
social learning required for self-renewal will be triggered.

Some colleagues have identified genuine decentralization as the basic requirement for the Canadian experiment
to succeed (Courchene, Segal, Rocher and Gilbert) while
others have argued in favour of decentralization as a sec-
ond-best (Peach), as more promising than the alternative
(Bélanger) or as the foundation of vibrant social learning
and self-renewal (Hubbard and Paquet).

In passing they have all denounced the same enemies of
decentralized federalism: the centralized mindset in good
currency (especially in Ottawa), an egalitarian ideology that
(by definition) trumps all other principles of social architecture, the myth of shared values (although on this a certain
schism has prevailed), the fixation on the need for someone
being in charge, and the impossibility of governing without
such a potentate.

Hopefully, we have slaughtered these sacred cows along
the way or at least put them out to pasture.

Optimisme mesuré

As to whether the decentralized federalism scenario will
prevail, our team can hardly be said to have come to a
common mind.

Three papers carry a strong whiff of pessimism.

Rocher and Gilbert are decisively pessimistic. What they feel is necessary for decentralization to prevail is nothing less than a cultural revolution that they regard as somewhat unlikely. Bélanger and Peach appear, on the surface, to be slightly more hopeful but their cautious endorsement of the decentralized federalism scenario has showcased in such vivid terms the logical and political forces standing in the way that one cannot extract more than a faint hope from their chapters.

The other three are clearly more optimistic.

Tom Courchene bases his optimism on the long history of successful creative social architecture that has accompanied the evolution of Canada since Confederation. Canadians are good examples of virtuous schemers who have been able to invent ways of governing themselves despite the anachronism of some founding documents. Hubbard and Paquet are optimistic because of the change in the context that is in the process of forcing all nation-states to revamp their governance. The pressure to transform will be such and the new tools so powerful that their presumption is strong that the drift toward decentralized federalism will prevail despite politicians, bureaucrats or witch doctors.

Hugh Segal's paper is more in the nature of a manifesto. It exudes optimism and brandishes as its main lever a principle mentioned by all the other papers: the principle of subsidiarity.

We have travelled quite a long distance in our thinking about federalism in Canada, except maybe in public administration academies. One of us remembers a meeting held in Toronto some twenty years ago with eminent federalism experts in which one of those leading experts took particular care to ridicule the idea that one might ever see subsidiarity as an organizing idea take hold on federalism issues. Can you ever envisage the citizens, he wryly suggested, taking to the street and chanting 'subsidiarity forever'?

We cannot be sure about the chanting, or about the word subsidiarity, but about the spirit of subsidiarity and the crucial importance of a confederal culture if this country is to survive, there is no doubt that the citizenry is already there! On these matters, it is the credentialized community of Canadian federalism experts that is culturally lagging.

Envoi

The traditionalists' efforts to drown federalism issues in the well of arcane constitutional language and intergovernmental wrangling may be coming to an end. The advantages of the few referenda of the last decades are that they have awakened the citizenry to the reality that it has a right and a responsibility to have a view on such matters as how their country should be run. Until now, Canadians have been polite and characteristically patient in waiting for questions to be put to them. We may be entering an age where they will start questioning dominant assumptions and demand to be heard.

Social movements begin when relations of power are seen "not as natural and inevitable, but as specific and changeable". This leads to public questioning that by "putting new questions on the agenda... opens up new possibility for political action" (Angus 2001: 73–74). Deep ecology had no more drawing power than subsidiarity in 1973, and yet...

References

Anderson, Walter T. 2001. *All Connected Now*. Boulder: Westview Press.

Angus, Ian 2001. *Emergent Publics*. Winnipeg: Arbeiter Ring Publishing.

Gigerenzer, Gerd 2002. "The Adaptive Toolbox." In *Bounded Rationality: The Adaptive Toolbox*, eds. G. Gigerenzer and R. Selten. Cambridge, MA: The MIT Press, 37–50.

Hasenclever, Andreas et al. 1997. *Theories of International Regimes*. New York: Cambridge Press.

Hock, Dee 1995. "The Chaordic Organization: Out of Control and Into Order." *World Business Academy Perspectives*, 9: 1: 5–18.

Kohr, Leopold (Hans) 1941. "Disunion Now: A Plea for a Society Based on Small Autonomous Units." *The Commonweal* (September 26).

Kohr, Leopold 1978. *The Overdeveloped Nations—The Diseconomies of Scale.* New York: Shocken Books.

Krasner, Stephen P. 1993. *International Regimes.* Ithaca: Cornell University Press.

Paquet, Gilles 1996–1997 "The Strategic State." *Ciencia Ergo Sum,* 3: 3: 257–261 (Part I); 4: 1: 28–34 (Part 2); 4: 2: 148–154 (Part 3).

Paquet, Gilles 2000. "André Laurendeau et la démocratie des communautés. " *Les Cahiers d'histoire du Québec au XXe siècle,* 10 : 45–54.

Paquet, Gilles 2008. *Gouvernance : mode d'emploi.* Montreal: Liber.

Paquet, Gilles 2009. "La difficile émergence d'une gouvernance mondiale baroque." *Télescope,* 15: 2: 105–117.

Raymond, Eric S. 2001. *The Cathedral and the Bazaar.* Cambridge, MA: O'Reilly

Polski, Margaret M. 2008. *Wired for Survival.* Upper Saddle River, NJ: FT Press.

Index

"f" refers to figure; "n" to notes; "t" to tables

centralized, highly, 15
centralized *vs.* decentralized, 127–28
centrifugal forces in, 25
civil-law, 15–16
common-law, 16
intra-state, 23
parliamentary, 15
presidential, 15
Federation of Saskatchewan Indian Nations (FSIN), 52–53
Finance Canada, 76f3.2–76f3.3, 101, 107–8, 114
First Ministers Conferences, 111
First Ministers' Meetings (FMM), 23–24
First Nations
communities, 104
federal government and its Constitutional mandates to, 111
federal policy management, 105
federal-provincial fiscal planning debates, 102
health benefits to people off reserve, 59
income levels, low, 109
policies, 105
Section 91 (24): Indians and lands reserved for the Indians, 59
self-government agreement, 52
separation of nation and state, 29
social welfare for off reserve, 59
socio-economic conditions in Saskatchewan, 53
socio-economic disadvantaged, 53

Fiscal Federalism (Oates), 17, 19, 42, 74, 89
Flaherty, Hon. James, 108
Fleiner, Thomas, 5, 10, 16
FMM. *See* First Ministers' Meetings
Forget, Claude, 30, 42
francophone Quebec scholars, 123
freedom-based organization, 7
free trade, 80, 107
French-speaking writers, 123
Friedman, Milton, 72, 89
Friedrich, Carl, 27, 42, 126, 147, 155
FSIN. *See* Federation of Saskatchewan Indian Nations

GAINS. *See* Guaranteed Annual Income Supplement for Seniors
GATT. *See* General Agreement on Tariffs and Trade
General Agreement on Tariffs and Trade (GATT), 80
German Basic Law, 39
Germany, 15, 39, 68, 76f3.2–76f3.3
Gigerenzer, Gerd, 212, 214
Gilles, Willem, 189, 201
Gladwell, Malcolm, 188, 201
Global Future for Canada's Global Cities (Courchene), 20, 42
globalization, 19, 109, 198, 206
Global Paradox (Naisbitt), 163, 201
Gomery's Blinders and Canadian Federalism (Hubbard and Paquet), 176, 201
"Gouvernance et déconcertation" (Paquet), 170, 202
governance. *See also* federalism
collaborative, 6, 159, 180, 190
defined, 1
polycentric, 1–3, 9, 160, 163
principles and tools of, 6

Governance Series Publications